C000145469

SHOW TIME!

A GUIDE TO MAKING EFFECTIVE PRESENTATIONS

THIRD EDITION

ELIZABETH P. TIERNEY

Published by Oak Tree Press, Cork T12 XY2N, Ireland.
www.oaktreepress.com / www.SuccessStore.com

© 2023 Elizabeth P. Tierney

Illustrations and original cover design by Aileen Caffrey.
Cover image this edition by alphaspirit / 123rf.com.
Cover design this edition by Kieran O'Connor Design.

A catalogue record for this book is available from the British Library.

ISBN 978-1-78119-561-1 Paperback
ISBN 978-1-78119-562-8 PDF
ISBN 978-1-78119-563-5 ePub
ISBN 978-1-78119-564-2 Kindle

CONTENTS

FOREWORD

Show Time! is a delightful read! As someone who's been talking for a living for nearly 40 years, I learned far more from this book than I expected to. This is a book anyone, regardless of experience, who wants to learn to be more efficient, effective, and impactful in public presentations, should absolutely read.

Before becoming a college dean 12 years ago, I was an economics professor for 25 years and have given hundreds of conference presentations, talks to the community, and more informal speeches at public events. I thought I fully "got it" when it comes to public speaking. What I didn't get was that there are so many aspects of preparing a presentation, not just giving it, you have to think about. Seemingly unimportant things, for example, like how you dress, rehearsing your presentation, how you prepare notes (Dr. Tierney has convinced me you *must* use notes), how you use your voice, how you plan for handling questions, even making sure you check out the mic in advance, are far more substantive in importance than you think.

My most insightful takeaway from this book is that YOU are responsible for your audience – not them, not your host, only you. If you take responsibility for your audience, focusing on who they are, what they need, how they can warm to you, and how your presentation can make a difference in their lives, this is the key to a successful presentation.

Dr. Tierney's chapter on handling your nerves is also very valuable. We all get varying degrees of stage fright, and she provides some great tips on how to overcome cases of the nerves.

From the President of the United States on down to a teen's class presentation in junior high, *Show Time!* is the most comprehensive, practical, and fun-to-read book on public speaking I've ever seen.

Örn Bodvarsson
Dean of the Atkinson Graduate School of
Management
Willamette University, Salem, OR.

Chapter 1
INTRODUCTION

"I often tell the story of the first time I gave a speech.
I was so nervous that I kept my eyes closed through
most of the monologue. I kept hoping that if I didn't
look at them, they would quietly go away. When I had
finished, I opened my eyes and discovered that,
unfortunately, my wish had been granted. There was
only one person left in the audience. He was a bookish-
looking fellow wearing a sour expression. Hoping to find
some solace in this catastrophe, I asked him why he
stayed. Still frowning, he replied, 'I'm the next speaker.'"

Victor Kiam, American businessman

"I'll be OK."
"I'll be fine."
"It'll be over soon."

These words may sound like the mutterings of a hospital
patient who is being wheeled into the operating room.
Actually, they are the same reassurances that you might
give yourself when you are introduced as the next
speaker at a meeting, or when you enter a room, stare at
the empty lectern, or at the camera and realize that you
are next – it's show time!

Then, the medical analogy falls apart. In the operating
room, you lie on the table while skilled, competent
professionals work on you. If you are speaking, however,
you are doing the work; you are not anaesthetized; you

are not prone. You are wide-awake and dependent on your own skills and competence, not on someone else's. Like the poor unfortunate on the trolley, you are worried. And being nervous is normal. Standing before an audience can be a scary experience. How scary? Well, the results of a survey conducted some years ago indicated that public speaking was perceived to be the second most frightening experience in your life. What was number one, you ask? Dying!

Why is making a presentation so terrifying? There are good reasons: you are alone, you are unprotected, you are vulnerable to attack, you are standing in front of other people who are looking at you and who expect something from you – great things. No matter how much ego you have, you are convinced that you will go blank, make a fool of yourself, and look bad in the eyes of your colleagues, friends, subordinates, prospective partners or superiors. The people in that audience will judge what you know and evaluate you. No wonder it is unnerving!

While you are trying to reassure yourself like the hospital patient and failing to do so, you are also undermining what confidence you may have by asking yourself questions like: Will I sound stupid? Will I get the job? The client? The referral? The loan? The approval? Will I be promoted? Relegated? Thanked? Ignored? Humiliated? Such a barrage of questions produces anxiety. Remember this is self-inflicted. You are doing it to yourself. We do it to ourselves.

Making a presentation need not be disquieting, daunting or terrifying. In fact, it can be exhilarating. The ideas and recommendations in this book are written to help you realize that although worrying is normal, you can get past the fear. Effective presentation is not a gift from the gods to a select few. It is not a mystery. It is a process and a product. With increased awareness and some simple techniques, anyone can learn to hold an audience's attention.

Knowing these techniques will help develop your strengths and diminish your weaknesses as a speaker. If you understand and accept some underlying assumptions and recommendations, if you practice and seek feedback, if you ask key preliminary questions, you will be confident, polished and self-aware. You will be someone whose ideas are considered, whose recommendations are weighed and who will earn the plaudits of the audience. In time, nervous but not terrified, you may seek opportunities to speak in public rather than dreading them. You may even enjoy influencing people.

By the end of this chapter, you will have read four recommendations underlying successful presentations; subsequent chapters will address specific strategies and techniques, Although each topic is dealt with separately for analytical purposes, each is an integral part of talking to a group.

Each chapter focuses on an aspect of presentation, from a brief review of the communication process, organizing your speech, using your voice, non-verbal language, notes and visuals to handling your nerves and questions. And recognizing the seismic shift in work brought about by the Covid-19 pandemic, we also consider online presentations. This book is designed to help you become a more comfortable, believable speaker, online or in person, not an unethical or deceitful one. As we know, taken to an extreme, effective speaking and image management can hide or distort the truth.

Before we begin, let's examine some more concerns about speaking, because airing them is healthy. You may recognize yourself in some of the worries I have heard expressed in workshops, and you may feel better knowing that you are not the only one who has these self-doubts. Even public figures and other people accustomed to speaking feel uneasy when they are facing an audience. I have spoken before audiences for years and still I worry.

So, what are we so anxious about? Sounding stupid? Convinced that the audience knows more about the subject than we do? Boring people to death? Forgetting what we planned to say? Freezing? Muddling up the content? All of the above? This self-talk undermines our confidence, whether we are part of a webinar, at a dinner, an interview, a class, at a board, department, a virtual sales meeting or pitching an idea to community leaders or bank officers.

Behind those nagging questions lurks the real issue. In our hearts, we know that it is not just our talk that is being judged. We are. Somehow, we think we will be found wanting: our names, our funding, our opportunity for advancement, our reputation, or our credibility is at stake. With that baggage, no wonder that surgery appears to be more pleasant than speaking. At least with a general or local anesthetic, we could sleep through the proceedings, or minimize the pain.

Speakers often reveal their discomfort by what they say when they are finished: "What a relief!" "Well, I am glad that's over" or "I survived." Notice, not "great!" or "excited" or "That went well." Rather than settle for survival, I urge you to turn the experience around and focus on the positive implications of giving a talk, the opportunities it affords you and your audience.

This book is written to assist you in being more at ease with the process and with yourself and – forgive me, Michael Porter – to give you a competitive advantage. You will interview better, run meetings smoothly, talk to clients effectively, give after-dinner speeches comfortably and sell your ideas convincingly.

Technology is invaluable and problematic. We rely on it and are exhausted by it. Despite our ever-increasing dependence, we still should be able to communicate face-to-face, individually and in groups, in person or remotely. The more at ease you are as a speaker, the more opportunities you create for yourself or for your organization and the more influential you can be.

What is written here is based on years of coaching teachers, trainers, students and businesspeople, as well as on my own experience as a speaker, trainer, and lecturer. It is based on the mistakes I have made and the lessons I have learned and continue to learn.

For one, I will never forget that dark day when one of my own dreaded fears was realized: I took one look at the lens of the camera in front of me and, despite my planning, remembered nothing. My mind was a complete blank. I froze.

I also remember the occasion when I paused during a speech and sensed the power to influence as the audience waited for my next words.

I have learned from attending meetings and conferences and from observing speakers, and from watching the audience's reactions to those speakers. I have seen individuals nod off, stare out the window or scroll through messages on their phones. I have also noted the eager looks of people who are engaged in what they are hearing.

To repeat, these pages are written with the conviction that you *can* learn to be a good presenter, to be less nervous, to have greater impact on the people listening to you and thus, affect your own growth and aid you in achieving goals for yourself and your organization.

My Four Recommendations

Let's begin by looking at four recommendations that apply to all presentations. They are:

1. Be responsible to the audience.

2. Make conscious decisions about what you are presenting rather than relying only on your intuition.

3. Make decisions before, during and after you speak.

4. Become aware of your own strengths and weaknesses as a presenter and practice using techniques that will enhance your talk.

Let's look at each these recommendations in more depth.

Be Responsible to the Audience

Speaking is about the audience. Frequently, as speakers, we are so self-absorbed that we forget about the people in front of us. We behave like primary school students who have been told to memorize a poem to recite in class. Remember how each student got up and raced through the poem, eyes glued to the floor, unaware of books falling, doors slamming, or classmates tittering?

Have you ever heard a presenter use the phrase, "Thank you for listening"? To me it is a revealing expression because it suggests that the audience made the effort when, in fact, the speaker was working on their behalf. If you do all the essential preparation and assume responsibility for being interesting, motivating, challenging, articulate, and/or entertaining, then the audience will listen and express their gratitude to you, thanking you for the effort you made for them. They will listen to you, if you are clear, sensitive, and analytical and seek to determine what will work for that unique group in front of you. As you know, time is a valuable resource, and the audience is devoting part of theirs to hearing what you have to say. Speaking is not about you; it is about the audience.

Make Conscious Decisions

Make conscious decisions about what you are doing when you speak and avoid relying solely on your intuition. In other words, as important as your gut instincts are, use your head as well to advise you what to do. To be effective, think about every aspect of the talk, from what you are wearing, where and how you stand, how best to use your voice and if and how to use technology. Ask yourself if you are using PowerPoint because other speakers do. Are you wearing a blue tie because it was the first one you saw in the closet? Is your choice of virtual background appropriate? Do you stand behind the table or lectern, simply because it happens to be in the room? Are you being reactive or proactive?

Instead, I encourage you to ask yourself if the blue tie is right for this occasion, or is it too pastel or too bold? Are slides necessary? If so, what for and why? Should you stand behind the lectern, or should you have it moved or removed so you appear more accessible and open? Is the image of palm trees or spaceships behind you appropriate? In other words, consciously decide what is best to do on each separate occasion.

Make Decisions Before, During and After

This recommendation is also about your decision-making. I urge you to make decisions before, during and after you speak. No, not just about your choice of tie, the number of slides or the use of the lectern.

For example, suppose you have 30 minutes to speak. You should decide beforehand what information to include and what to exclude to fit within that time frame.

Then, during your speech, you may notice several audience members nodding off. If you accept my earlier recommendation, to assume responsibility for the audience, you know that you should re-engage those tired folks. What you do now requires immediate decisions, whether it is lowering your voice, raising it, cutting part of your talk, pounding on a table, or pausing. In that moment, you make a change.

When the talk is over, reflect on how your audience received your speech, how you felt, any questions you were asked, and any feedback you received. Weigh what you might have done differently, what you might have forgotten and analyze what worked. In that way you decide what to incorporate or exclude for the next talk.

Be Aware of Your Strengths and Weaknesses

Get to know your own strengths and weaknesses as a speaker and find opportunities to practice techniques that enhance your own presentation style. Ballet dancers, poets, athletes, and painters have talent; we forget that developing their art required learning and practicing techniques to enhance those gifts. It takes more than passion on the day to win an Olympic Gold or World Cup Final.

Actors and musicians need more than enthusiasm for their art to muster the energy for the 100th performance. Performers have a job to do, and they have years of experience and techniques to sustain them. While we may not be Grammy or Oscar winners, as presenters we need to understand that there are approaches that will enhance and support us. Discover what you are good at and what needs to be developed. Do you have a beautiful voice but speak too quickly? Do you avoid eye contact? Do you tend to speak off the cuff? Subsequent chapters will help you to identify your own strengths and weaknesses.

In Summary

While it is normal to be nervous before making a presentation, you should not be so terrified that you hurt yourself personally and professionally. To gain confidence, weigh the four recommendations that can make a difference in the quality of your work:

1. Be responsible to the audience.

2. Make conscious decisions about what you are presenting rather than relying only on your intuition.

3. Make decisions, before, during and after you speak.

4. Become aware of your own strengths and weaknesses as a presenter and practice using techniques that will enhance your talk.

You are on the way to being a more credible, clear and confident speaker. Before examining specific techniques that we have alluded to, let's step back and remind ourselves about the communication process itself.

Chapter 2
COMMUNICATING

"How well we communicate is determined not by how well we say things but by how well we are understood."
Andrew S. Grove, former CEO, Intel Corporation

"What we have here is a failure to communicate."
from the movie *Cool Hand Luke*

Let's take a moment and examine from a theoretical perspective what happens when we communicate. Doing that should enable you to analyze a process that is both instantaneous and that most of us take for granted. We do not think about it. This chapter is included to remind you of what we are doing when we speak and to highlight some of the difficulties that are inherent in the process of trying to share ideas. It should help you assess what you can do as a speaker to minimize these difficulties and to increase the odds of having your ideas understood and acted upon.

Basically, the two-way communication process requires a sender and a receiver. Some people compare the exchange to a tennis or ping-pong match. One author compared the communications process to the disassembling of London Bridge in England, stone by stone, and sending it across the Atlantic and reassembling it in Arizona.

The communication process involves a series of steps that begin when the sender has an idea or a feeling, a message, which may be a simple "Hello," a strategic business plan or an architectural design. Regardless of its complexity or level of abstraction, it is a message that emanates from the sender and is intended for the receiver.

The next step in the process belongs to the sender too. The idea or concept, the message, needs to be encoded before it is sent. The codes might be words, pictures, music, hand or even smoke signals. That coded message then needs to be transmitted in some way. Do you opt to write, sing, draw, dance, or text?

Assume you are the sender in this situation. You recognize a former colleague in a shopping mall. You want to greet her, so you encode your message with a signal: a gesture. You raise your hand and transmit the greeting by moving your upraised arm quickly from side to side – you wave at her. But your friend has moved into the next aisle.

You try a different code and means of transmission: words, spoken words. The original message remains unchanged, but you encode and transmit it differently. "Hello, Deirdre!" transmitted with words spoken loudly. Notice you said, "Hello," not "Bonjour." You opted for English, not French. But in the crowd of shoppers, you still were unable to get Deirdre's attention.

But you have her phone number, so that evening you continue encoding your message in English words. You phone her; she doesn't answer, so you leave a message on her voicemail. That fails, so you text. This time you lengthen the message: "Hi, Deirdre. Saw you at the mall. Sorry I missed you. Please text or phone me."

Days pass, and no word from Deirdre. Unwilling to give up, you send the message one more time – encoded again in English, but this time in writing – an email. "D. Trying to say 'Hello,' but keep missing you. Phoned on Monday. Left a message. Texted. Please phone me at the office."

The message, while longer, remains essentially "Hello." You have continued to use English, but you have varied your transmission from non-verbal language, the wave, to the spoken word, to voicemail and finally the written word, by text and email. Sad to say, despite your best efforts, Deirdre fails to respond. The critical next step in the communications process has not occurred. The message has not been received. You had a message that was encoded and transmitted, but two-way communication remains one-way unless the receiver acknowledges receipt.

Good news. Several days later, Deirdre phones you at work and begins with "Thanks for your email. My cell was acting up. Sorry I missed you. We need to catch up. Coffee this weekend?" With those words of Deirdre's, you now know she received the message, decoded it accurately and gave you feedback. She understood and did as you asked: she contacted you. Now it's your move again.

Examined this way, communicating is a straightforward process. Giving a talk, like a simple "Hello" to a colleague, involves the same steps: identifying the message, encoding it appropriately, and transmitting it so that the audience receives your ideas, decodes them, acts or does not act on them and gives you feedback. Simple. No problem.

Would that it was that easy. As you know, problems and barriers abound. Effective speakers are sensitive to the endless blockages in communication, because any one of them can have significant implications for your success in having your ideas received and/or acted upon. Let's look at some problems, starting as we did earlier with the initial message.

Have a Clear Message

Obviously, any topic that you plan to talk about is going to be far more sophisticated and complicated than "Hello" to a colleague in a mall.

Whatever the topic, think through the message carefully. Even if you encode it precisely and transmit it thoughtfully, without a clear initial message, the recipients may become confused. Remember the reference to London Bridge? It was dismantled, sent, received and reassembled. The only problem was that the purchaser thought he was buying the Tower Bridge. The message was confused – an expensive mistake. You have undoubtedly experienced similar problems with talks you have attended. Have you ever left a meeting after someone else's presentation saying, "What was that about?" or "Well, that was a waste of a morning!" or "What was the point of that?" These phrases are feedback and suggest that the message itself either was unclear or worthless to you as the listener. **Chapter 6** is designed to help you refine your thinking about the intent of your talk.

Select Your Words Carefully

Let's assume that you have worked out a clear message. Perhaps you plan to explain the implications of a new online recruiting system. Sounds good. Let's look at some encoding problems.

Earlier, you decided against sending a message to Deirdre in French – an easy decision because you knew Deirdre speaks only English. You should spend time thinking about the implications of your code choice, lest you select an inappropriate one. To make the point, it would be unlikely for you to translate your talk on the updated online recruiting system into Latin and intone it to the audience in a Gregorian chant, just as an architect would not write building plans for a contractor in iambic pentameter. Annual reports are not collections of family snapshots, nor does the ground crew at an airport email a pilot to indicate at which gate he should park the plane.

As absurd as these examples are, inadvertently we can make a silly encoding decision, too. For example, if you decide to encode your talk in a specialized language that is highly technical or germane only to specialists in fields that have their own vocabulary, such as medicine, insurance, law or information technology, members of the audience who are unfamiliar with that language will be unable to decipher your message. A similar problem might be your choosing to speak Dutch to an all French-speaking audience. In essence, selecting foreign or technical languages may be problematic. The audience may be unable to understand what you are saying, if your talk is filled with "jargon." Or are you using words and phrases like: throughputting, inputting, vertically challenging, synergizing, or moving goal posts? Like the contractor unable to visualize the building, or the pilot waiting in vain to park the aircraft, your audience may be unable to act on what you say if they are unfamiliar with your words.

Meaning itself may constitute another problem. Here are several examples:

"I thought you said two," remarked Tom. "No, I meant 'also,' not 'two'," said Bill.

I remember walking into a shop in Ireland and being asked, "Are you OK?" As an American, I immediately wondered if I was looking unwell. While "Are you OK?" is English, to me it meant something other than "May I help you?"

There was a famous comedy routine about the man who got a traffic ticket for making a U turn in a one-way street. He understood "NO U TURN" to mean "No, you turn."

While these are light-hearted examples, as a speaker, you should focus on the clarity of your primary message and also on the implications of the code, your word choices, if you want your message received as it was intended. So, let's suppose you have done your homework, and the message is meaningful and the code choice appropriate. What else might go wrong?

Understand Transmission Problems

Getting the message to the receiver may be another problem. Remember Deirdre? Perhaps the mall was crowded and noisy, so she neither saw you when you waved nor heard you when you spoke. You phoned her, and although you left her a voicemail, she might have been talking on the phone, or have turned it off, or had no service where she was. Had she answered, perhaps the call might have broken up, or you might have heard music or static on the line. Our poor pilot might receive the email about where to park but discover that the attachment is missing.

As a speaker, voicemail or blurred faxes are unlikely concerns; however, you may have other issues: street or construction noise, people walking by, phones ringing, or acoustics problems like echoes, or computers freezing, or microphones squealing or failing. And Zoom fatigue is real: staring at a screen without a break is exhausting physically and emotionally – yet another concern for you, as is the clarity of your speech pattern, your ability to project your voice, or the quality and choice of your visuals.

Anticipating and handling these problems is up to you because you are the sender of the message. You have control of the first three steps in the communications process: the message, the choice of code and its transmission.

Know Your Audience

Once you have transmitted your message, the control shifts to the receiver. Therein lie more potential problems for you as a speaker. Worst case? Suppose the receiver does not like you. No matter the pains you take to prepare, the receiver may interpret your message in terms of their perceptions of you. "There he goes, profiling again!" "Just trying to show the rest of us up."

Suppose rather than your personality, it's your values that are annoying. You may have a public view on climate change, religion, abortion, sexuality, or even on Manchester United, that the receivers find repugnant or offensive. So, your message may be rejected out of hand, even if the topic has nothing to do with any those issues.

You may not be the problem; the receiver may be. Deirdre may not have heard you because she was out of earshot, or she may have been pre-occupied, concerned with the time and eager to leave before the traffic became too heavy. In the same way, someone in your audience could be pre-occupied with a personal problem like a large payment due on a credit card bill or a deadline for a report that is fast approaching, or an excessively absent staff member who needs counseling. In other words, the receivers may admire you, but in the moment may be distracted from what you are saying by their own non-work or work-related issues. Given the volume of information we face today, distraction is a major problem for us as speakers because we are asking the audience to stay focused.

Let's complicate this speaking business even more. The receiver, your audience, processes information more quickly than you can speak, which means that no matter how interesting or relevant the subject matter, the receiver has the capability of listening to you and thinking about other issues simultaneously: planning holidays, what to have for lunch, picking up the dry cleaning, servicing the car, planning for an afternoon meeting, or scheduling a conference call. That mental capacity to handle more information than you alone can provide while speaking is a challenge for you. The solution is not to speak faster to fill up the space – it is to keep them engaged by being interesting, dynamic and relevant.

Earlier, we referred to the quality of visuals. Remember that, just like words, pictures send messages, and most speakers choose to include some visuals in their talks. Undoubtedly you have experienced examples of this kind of encoding and transmission problem: the font that is too small to read, the graph without labels, the chart with too many trends, the slide with too many bullet points, the photo that is too big for the screen, the images that are faded, distorted or reversed – concerns, worries, reasons to be nervous? No, not if you anticipate them.

The point of breaking the communication process into simpler components and highlighting some of the difficulties that may occur by looking at problems inherent in sending a simple greeting to a friend is to remind you of the importance of making conscious decisions about your message, your code, and your means of transmission in advance of any talk you give. You can see that learning about your receivers is invaluable and why it may be unwise to rely solely on your instincts and on your spontaneity. You know communication breaks down. If you are aware of potential problems, then you can plan and organize for them – not all perhaps, but many. That attention to detail is one of the hallmarks of a good speaker. In other words, by looking at the theoretical communication model, you may appreciate the need to:

- Have a clear message when you speak.
- Select your words, pictures and gestures thoughtfully.
- Transmit what you have to say clearly.
- Know your audience.

As a result, the receiver, your audience, will understand the implications of that new recruitment system so clearly that you will avoid 12 messages after your talk asking you questions about it, questions you already answered in your speech. Nor will you have to write additional emails or memos clarifying what you said the previous day.

In Summary

By having a better understanding of what is involved in the two-way communication process, the mystery about speaking should fade. Why you should be responsible for the audience becomes clearer, and your confidence should increase because you know what to do.

So far, we have focused on verbal language with a brief reference to the language of images. Now let's look at non-verbal language as a means of communicating. It is important for you, because while the audience is listening to your words and looking at the visuals, you are the focus of their attention.

Chapter 3
USING NON-VERBAL LANGUAGE

"We all, in one way or another, send our little messages to
the world ... and rarely do we send our messages
consciously. We act out our state of being with nonverbal
body language. We lift one eyebrow for relief. We rub our
noses for puzzlement. We clasp our arms to isolate
ourselves or to protect ourselves .... The gestures are
numerous, and while some are deliberate ... there are
some that are mostly unconscious."

Julius Fast, author of *Body Language*

This chapter is dedicated to two main issues:

- How your body and your choice of clothing may
  enhance your ability to get your message across.
- How, conversely, your body and choice of
  clothing may interfere with your audience's
  ability to receive, decode and act on the ideas
  that you have labored over for days or weeks.

We indicated that using jargon, poor listening or noise
may impact communication; our non-verbal language
can affect it too. To increase your awareness of the
impact of non-verbal language on your audience, the
first step is to recognize the messages that certain types
of body language may send to an audience. You may
recognize some of your own patterns. Be pleased with

your good ones, and work on eliminating any gestures or actions that detract from your performance. If you think you have several, then pick one to work on first, then another, if need be. You will feel frustrated if you tackle too many at once. Every diet book tells you to focus on the success of losing one pound at a time, not on the fact that you have 10 to go before you reach your desired weight.

So, let's look at some of the physical aspects of presentation – what the audience sees: your head, your face, your arms and hands, your gestures and stance, your legs and your feet – the last three not so much virtually. Let's see how your use of them may interfere with your audience's ability to concentrate on your words and then consider what you might do to reinforce your words by using more appropriate non-verbal messages. To restate the earlier point, your physical aspects of presentation should reinforce your message, not interfere with it.

An extreme example is the habit some folks have of speaking with one hand over their mouths. Obviously, that gesture prevents the audience from understanding or even hearing the speaker. Some people do that and are not aware that they do. As you read, see if you notice some of your own idiosyncrasies or those of speakers you have seen.

Please, as I said, do not beat yourself up if you recognize five or six. To repeat, pick one and try to change that one. Then, after you have made headway, pick another one and work on it. Neymar or David Beckham did not master all the techniques in one day or one week. It takes time, effort, patience and a pat on the back. And do give yourself that pat on the back!

Your Head and Face

Beginning at the top of your body and working down: heads move up and down and side to side. If, as you speak, you let your head wobble, you may look like a large creature, like *Sesame Street*'s Big Bird. Some people, usually more women than men, deliver their entire talk with their heads tilted to one side; they appear to be demure or coquettish, or wistfully begging for support or sympathy. If your talk is about the implications of downsizing – a serious subject – and through the entire speech, you have your head tilted to one side, with your shoulder raised to meet it, you may look coy or kittenish, not exactly the look for a captain of industry or determined entrepreneur. So, too, if you hold your head up with your chin aloft, you risk looking arrogant.

Imagine, too, shaking your head from side to side to signify what many cultures recognize as "No," and yet saying "Yes," how "delighted" you are to be speaking on this occasion. Or you shake your head, up and down, "Yes," when you are saying: "There is definitely no problem with our emissions." Keep your head in a comfortable neutral position and move it naturally. In other words, be sure your movement is not sending one message while your words are sending another, a mixed message: "Yes" with your words, and "No" with your head, or "Yes" with your head and "No" with your words. Notice how something as simple as how you hold your head may make you appear timid or smug when all you want is to be straightforward.

Facial expressions, too, may cause problems. It's remarkable how many speakers look grim – no matter what the subject. Like your head movement, your facial expression should reinforce your message. Let your face light up, smile, and look happy. When you say, "Good morning" or "Good afternoon," a look of genuine pleasure is warranted, even if you are nervous. If you are "pleased with the outcome of the study," if you are "delighted with the recommendations," if you are "excited at the prospect," then, for heaven's sake, look pleased, delighted or excited. That does not mean that you should wear a grin from ear to ear for the duration of the talk, nor should you smile if you are saying that you are "concerned" with the findings, "worried" about the non-compliance, "disturbed" by the competition. Your face should mirror your words.

Because you are likely to be more nervous at first, you will probably have no difficulty looking worried, and it may be harder to look cheerful. But smiling helps you feel better. Try it. The warmth you emit has an impact on the audience. Remember the experience when you walked into classes or doctors' offices? How did you feel when you were greeted by a smiling professional instead of one who was tight-lipped and intense? You can produce the same feelings in your audience. Your expression affects their level of interest or motivation. Smiles work wonders.

Your Eyes

You are holding your head up and trying to smile at appropriate times. What about those eyes? Yes, we all know that we should make eye contact. Let's think about why. Ask yourself if you genuinely look at people and see what you are looking at? Really see. Strive to look at every face in the audience, not over their heads to the back, out a window, or to the upper left-hand corner of the room or screen.

By looking at each face, you are signaling to the audience that you like them, that you have nothing to hide, that you are honest, open and direct. And by looking and seeing those faces and reactions, you get immediate feedback, a critical dimension in the two-way communication process. Remember that Deirdre didn't give us feedback until she finally returned the call.

In **Chapter 4,** you will learn what to do with what you see. For the moment, let's stay with the looking. When you look at everyone, avoid starting at the left side of the room and moving your head and eyes methodically to the right, or starting at the right and scanning to the left like a periscope in search of a target.

Instead, look at everyone randomly – even in a room of 400 people (on Zoom, look at the camera). And "everyone" means just that, not only the person whom you perceive to have the power – the one with the title. Even Don Corleone, the Godfather, had a *consigliore*. In other words, be careful about assuming that the CEO, the President, the Chair, or the Department Head make unilateral decisions. People in power seek advice from other people, and those individuals may be in attendance. If you disregard someone, you risk alienating him or her.

Another reason for looking at faces is because, when you look at someone, the person usually returns the glance. Thus, you encourage people to pay attention. You are also sending the message that you value everyone in the room. Everyone is important. A second or two on a face is enough.

One *caveat*: Beware of the "nodder." Often someone appears to be hanging on your every word and nodding in agreement. A friend! An ally! Thank goodness! You may be nervous, so you are grateful for some reassurance. As a speaker, when you are feeling vulnerable, it is easy to lock your eyes onto that nodding head like a guided missile. Without meaning to, you may begin to direct your talk to that individual to the neglect of the others in the room. While you may have successfully developed a relationship with one person, the others may stop listening and quietly resent your neglect.

Sometimes the seating arrangement may influence you. One side may have more people than the other. Catch yourself if you notice you are ignoring the smaller group. Try to involve everyone by making an effort to look and to see.

Your Body

Moving down from your head and face, what about those appendages connected to your shoulders – your arms? And those additional bits at the end – your hands? What a nuisance they are for most of us. Where did those hands come from? What should I do with them?

Just as you have seen poor visuals, you have also witnessed all the attempts by speakers to solve the arm-hand problem. Do these examples sound familiar? Speakers who:

- Glue their arms to their sides and look like trees or totem poles.
- Clasp them behind their backs to be rid of them.
- Put one hand or both hands in their pockets, sometimes, playing with their coins or keys to appear nonchalant.
- Cross their arms across their chests, place their hands together in prayer, or lower them to protect other vulnerable parts.

None of these solutions is ideal. Instead of looking open and confident, the speaker is signaling to the audience a level of discomfort by appearing stiff, insecure, scared, or defensive. While we may feel that way, what we want is for our non-verbal message to be one of strength, openness and honesty.

So, what do you do? Your non-verbal language should reinforce your verbal one. You are your own living visual. You should use your head, hands and arms to assist you communicating your ideas. True, it takes practice to unglue that arm from your side or take your hand out of a pocket. You want to use them the way you do when you are having a casual conversation. To become more self-aware, the next time you chat with a friend, watch how both of you use your hands to make a point. Notice too how useful your fingers are for counting or clarifying: "The three advantages of ...," or "Two reasons why ... ."

Be careful about scripting your movements. By that I mean deciding in advance to touch your chest every time you use the word, "I," or pointing to the audience every time you say "you." You risk looking robotic or like a marionette. In other words, talk conversationally and use your hands naturally; if something you are describing is large, show how large with your hands; if it is heavy, heft it. How do you describe the salmon you caught? With your hands.

Be wary of wringing your hands, particularly if the subject of your talk is financial. Rather than appearing to be a businessperson, you may look like Charles Dickens' Fagin delighting over a pickpocketed watch. Avoid pointing with your finger, pen, pointer, or remote. It may be perceived as a threatening gesture and may offend, so use an open hand.

To reiterate, use your entire body to reinforce your message and to emphasize your points. That is true for your head and arms and for your legs, your feet and your overall stance. Unless you are an actor in a grade B cowboy movie, try to keep both hips even, rather than having one up and one down.

When you walk up to the front of the room or onto the dais, stand with assurance. Plant each foot in a line directly below each of your shoulders and hips to support your weight evenly. If you press both feet tightly together, you may appear to be on the verge of toppling over, and your audience might be waiting for you to do just that. Some speakers assume dance positions with their legs and feet and look as if they are ready to break into a tango or cha-cha. Some speakers rock from side to side or roll up on their toes and then down on their heels. Still others cross their ankles or bend them as if they were learning to ice skate. Remember you want to appear strong, open and confident, not like the leaning tower of Pisa or an extra in an early spaghetti western, with your hips and shoulders akimbo, hands in your pockets.

You can and should move, if space permits. Feel free to walk but not like a lion pacing in a confined space. Move around. Speak from the right, walk to the left, if it is appropriate or warranted. Your movement creates interest, energizes you and your talk, and helps keep the audience engaged.

Standing up straight, chest high, shoulders relaxed supports your voice. Because you can breathe more deeply, it will be stronger, and good posture helps you maintain eye contact better. It is easy to lean on furniture, to welcome any kind of support, even if it is from a wooden lectern. But if you do, the audience may think you are tired, lazy, too casual or frightened, so avoid holding on to desks or resting against furniture.

By the way, a big person with a loud voice, leaning in toward the audience may appear aggressive and therefore off-putting. Stand tall with your legs supporting you and feel free to move around. Initially your heart may be pounding faster than you like, but you will look and sound self-assured.

And posture matters virtually as well. Make sure you are sitting or standing up straight, looking into the camera with a few inches of headspace. Some folks reveal no faces and only show the top of their heads because they are comfortably leaning back in a soft chair or sofa.

There is one additional category of non-verbal messages we should discuss and that is idiosyncratic gestures. Pay attention to see if you have any movements that are distracting: tossing your head to get the bangs out of your eyes, scratching your cheek, or pulling your ear. There is nothing wrong with any of these gestures. We are human, after all, and they are normal, but when any one is repeated too often, the audience may begin to notice. Only then do the gestures become problematic. What happens is that your listeners begin to focus on the frequency with which you smooth your tie, fix your hair, play with a button, or push your glasses up onto your nose than to your calculations about your company's market share.

Your Clothing

Since we mentioned a tie earlier, let's talk about your choice of clothing. If you think of presenting a talk in terms of the theatre, then your clothes are your costume. They reflect who you are, so select your outfit thoughtfully. What you wear should match the occasion and the tone you want to set. You want the audience to pay attention to what you are saying rather than to how you move and what you are wearing. The audience will most likely not notice your choice of brown shoes, but they may notice unpolished ones. They may notice if you have a tear in a jacket or a missing button. Gentlemen, they may notice holes in the ankles of your socks. Ladies, are there runs in your stockings? Minor flaws, but you risk the audience's thinking that, if you are sloppy about those details, perhaps you will be careless about the ideas that you are discussing.

I recall seeing a speaker wearing a raincoat during her entire talk. True, the room was chilly, but I overheard people wondering if she was in a hurry to leave – not the ideal message to send.

Choose comfortable clothing. Wear outfits that are problem-free. Avoid shirts or blouses with collars that choke you, shoes that pinch so much your feet hurt, buttons that slip open, scarves that slide off your shoulders, skirts that ride up or slacks that slip down. (Yoga socks on Zoom may be just fine!)

Pick what looks best on you and fits you well. Pass on the trousers with the bottoms that bunch around your ankles, the jacket with sleeves that are so long they cover your hands. Men, if the occasion calls for a shirt and tie, be sure the collar of the shirt closes, and select a tie that remains knotted and that will stay comfortably at the neck to cover that collar button. Women, consider how you are wearing your hair and your choice of jewelry. Will your earrings be the center of attention, or will your message?

Before you are announced, while you are in your seat or still "backstage," make any minor necessary adjustments to your clothing. Tuck in a shirt or blouse, straighten a tie, button a button and then let it go. Once you are in full view of the audience, just like playing with your glasses, adjusting your clothing may become a distraction. Forgive the familiarity, but if you find yourself hiking up your pants or pulling up a wayward bra strap, you may want to rethink your choices for next time.

What colors should you select? What styles should you wear? Those are your decisions to make. You know what makes you look and feel good, and there are articles on color and style for your skin tones and build. Certain fashions and colors look better on some people than on others. Decide whether a double-breasted suit is the most flattering for your height and weight. Is this a sport shirt and jeans occasion? Or suits and ties? You need not run to the store and buy the latest fashion. Wear what is comfortable, neat, not distracting and appropriate for the occasion.

Speaking of color, if purple is this year's color, but it is not yours, don't wear it; select another color that looks good on you. If I wear pale yellow or light green, I look as if a trip to the doctor's office is in order. High contrast like black against white or navy against white gives you an image of higher authority. Charcoal grey against a light background is another good combination. Blue and yellow or beige and blue are softer and friendlier. You might consider wearing brighter colors on drearier days – at a talk on Tuesday after a public holiday, or on a Monday morning. What you wear is another pre-speaking decision. And single colors rather than large patterns tend to be less distracting on Zoom.

Finding the right "costume" may be harder for women than for men: long skirt, short skirt, slacks, pant suit, slit skirt and so on. The fuchsia mohair sweater, the see-through blouse with the décolletage, the three-inch earrings, or the skirt "for standing only" may not be right for the day. Each item in and of itself may be stunning on you, but if you are delivering a serious message that has implications for you or for an organization you represent, you want to be sure that the audience is focused on your face, your words, your visuals, your message, not on how attractive you are, or how clever those earrings may be. And wear comfortable shoes!

You look good. You have selected clothes that do not distract. Make one more decision: how do you want to wear your hair. Will your hair fall into your eyes? Are your bangs too long? We have all seen men and women who appear to have only one eye or spend time throughout their talk fighting that wayward strand of hair that keeps falling out of place.

If you own a watch, wear it. If not, be sure you know where there is a clock in the room, have your phone nearby or check your iPad or laptop – if you are using one. We will talk more about the importance of time later, but you want to be able to see that you are on schedule.

Enthusiasm

Care about what you are saying, even if you have given your talk 10 or 15 times before. It is new to the audience, so it needs to sound fresh. No matter how tired you are of the weekly induction meeting or plea to the next banker for a loan, you need to be passionate in your delivery and your subject. Your enthusiasm can be contagious – in the best sense of the word.

In Summary

You have a lot to think about because you are sending non-verbal messages along with your verbal ones. Think about how you use your body, your head, your face, your arms and hands, the way you stand and move and how you dress on the day. There are no absolutes, no rules. You may decide that you are deliberately not going to smile throughout the entire talk, or that you want to take off your jacket and roll up your sleeves, or that you will sit on the table, or wear the tie that looks like a fish or the stockings with sequins at the ankles. Fine! If you do, presumably you decided that doing any or all of these things will have the desired impact on your audience and will send them on their way remembering your message.

Chapter 4
USING YOUR VOICE

"Proper words in proper places make the true
definition of a style."
Jonathan Swift

By now, you may be wondering how you are ever going to remember all this advice – look pleasant, but not all of the time; look at people's faces, but not for too long; use your hands to emphasize points, but not too often; stand tall and walk, but avoid pacing. You haven't even begun to organize your talk yet. Before you start drafting it; however, let's examine two more physical aspects of presentation: your voice and speech patterns. They can have a significant impact on your audience.

Many speakers take their voices for granted and fail to take advantage of what their voices can do; they undervalue them. Certainly, you could take speech or elocution lessons, but there is much that you can consider on your own. As before, the first step in the process involves awareness, recognizing what you can do with your voice and speech pattern to take advantage of their potential for turning an OK talk into an excellent one.

Pacing

Let's consider the speed at which you talk, the pace. If you accelerate and decelerate, you can be more interesting. Most people speak too quickly when they first stand up to talk in front of a group. Why? You know the answer. We speak more quickly when we are nervous, and because we want to get the ordeal over with as quickly as possible, so we rush. Remember that notion of being responsible to that audience? They need to be able to comprehend what you are saying. Because they are unable to engage you in conversation in the moment and say, "Would you mind clarifying that last point?" or "Did I understand you to mean ...?", they are dependent on what you say and how you say it. So, you should speak slowly enough for them to capture the meaning without having to question you throughout the talk, because they can't.

Therefore, accepting that most of us are more nervous at the beginning of a talk than at the end of it, compensate for that discomfort by speaking your opening sentences more slowly than normal, thus, ensuring that your first words do not all run together. Have you ever heard someone open with "Goomorniniznicetobehere"? If that sounds like what it looks like, it will be hard to understand. If you continue in that vein, the people facing you will concentrate for a bit, but may give up trying to follow you. Their eyes may glaze over, and they may think of the other issues that they have to deal with.

Pausing

You can always stop. Frequently, in our eagerness to be done, we race through a talk like a bullet train. Take a more leisurely route and make some local stops. In other words, you can speed up through less important material and slow down through the nuts and bolts or the complicated portion and pause.

Pausing is an excellent technique because it gives the audience a chance to take in your words, to absorb them or to reflect on their import. Speakers frequently build rhetorical questions into their talks: "Why should you buy widgets?" But then they forget to give the audience time to think either about the question itself or about an answer.

Suppose a speaker has decided to startle the audience with a new concept to implement within the organization – perhaps the introduction of hybrid work scheduling. Rather than making the recommendation for the scheduling and pausing to permit the audience to get their heads around the idea, the speaker charges ahead into four justifications and six implications for the recommendation – each one of which may require some thought. What may happen is that while the speaker is on point number nine, the audience may still be thinking about the original notion – hybrid work scheduling.

If you plan to have time for questions at the end, you want the audience to be able to jot down some notes or questions as you speak. They will not be able to write anything if you are already talking about justification number four, and they are still processing numbers two and three. So, take your time and pause.

To repeat: slow down, particularly at the beginning, but also throughout the talk when you are making key points. Consider varying the pace – sometimes slow, sometimes fast and sometimes pause or stop altogether – not just for the sake of pausing or stopping, but because doing so alters the impact of your talk and affords the audience time to reflect. Speakers who vary their pace are more interesting to listen to, thus helping to eliminate any concern you might have about being boring.

Accents

Suppose you come from another part of the city, the country or the world than where you are speaking – born in Ireland, speaking in Detroit. You may have an accent that is unfamiliar to the audience. If they are unused to certain sounds, they may have difficulty decoding at first, so, once again, take your time. Give the audience a chance to adjust to the way you pronounce certain sounds. They will, in time.

People who have heavy regional accents are sometimes advised to rid themselves of them. If you have one but are understood by others, please don't change. Audiences welcome the difference. If, however, you realize that there is a particular sound that you make that may confuse or change the meaning of what you are saying, then work on that single sound. Avoid puzzling your audience as to whether you said "three" or "tree." Again, slow down and allow the audience to adjust and enjoy.

Pitch

You are more interesting to listen to if you vary the pitch of your voice. The word "monotone" means just that – one sound. Your voice, like a musical instrument, has a range. By raising or lowering the pitch, you avoid that "poor Johnny-one-note" quality. None of us speaks all the time as a basso, an alto or a soprano. In English, our voices go up at the end of a sentence to signal to the listener that we are asking a question. In other words, we can alter the pitch. Don't you agree? If you say, "Don't you agree?" aloud, notice the change of pitch.

Volume

In addition to pacing and pitch, add volume to your list of variables. We are like a sound system. We can speak softly or loudly as well as somewhere in between. We have whispered to a friend sitting beside us at the movies and shouted with pleasure or dismay during a match. We are raising and lowering the volume. Add that to your repertoire. Creating verbal diversity makes you more compelling.

"But I usually speak softly," you might say. Slow down and stand tall, look out, breathe deeply through your nose and project your voice to the back of the room, not at the table in front of you or at the first row of the audience. You will be heard.

Projecting

A bit more about projecting. In **Chapter 3**, we indicated that maintaining eye contact is an important skill, and I referred to looking and seeing. Have you ever heard a speaker ask the question, "Can you hear me in the back?" Why, oh, why, do speakers ask it? Courtesy? True, how can you be sure that those in the back of the room can hear you if you don't have a mic?

If you are giving your talk in a large room, and you are worried about not being heard, one simple technique is to imagine that your grandma is seated in the back row; her hearing is not what it was, and she is not wearing a hearing aid. Project your voice to the back and direct your preliminary remarks to your imaginary grandma and to the people on either side of her. When you speak your opening sentences, look at those people and gauge their reactions. You can quickly determine whether or not they can hear you. How can you tell? Watch *their* non-verbal language.

They will give you feedback by leaning toward you or turning their heads so that their ears are directed toward you, indicating that they are straining to hear, or the looks on their faces may reveal their reactions to your words, thus indicating that they can or cannot hear you. Please don't ask "Can you hear me in the back?" Read the reaction without asking. Raise the volume or keep it where it is.

And, by the way, how would their answer help? "No" means they heard you ask the question, while "Yes" means the same. All speakers do by asking that question is to disrupt the flow of the talk, particularly at that critical starting point. But then again, asking "Can you hear me in the back?" may be a clever opening for a talk on "Hearing and Listening."

So, in the opening moments of your talk, in addition to making a conscious effort to adjust your volume, pace and pitch, project your voice to your grandma or grandpa in the back.

Extraneous Noises and Pet Phrases

Some of us make unnecessary sounds when we speak. To discover if you do, seek the help of a friend or record yourself. Speak on any subject for a few minutes. Ask for feedback or listen for any extraneous noises that you may be making when you talk. Or ask your colleague if you repeat specific sounds. You may discover that you have the habit of saying "em" or "er" between words when you pause. You may make "tsk" or clicking sounds like some African singers because of the way you press your tongue against the roof of your mouth. You may smack your lips. No, it is not the end of the world if you do make any or all of those sounds, but like the other physical aspects of presentation, too many "er"s or "tsk"s may be distracting. What do you do to stop? Just like idiosyncratic gestures, become aware of the habit, catch yourself in the act and try to avoid doing it the next time.

You will. Slowly and steadily, the noises will disappear. You will replace the old habit with a new one – silence between words.

Besides making "tsk" and "er" sounds, some speakers "sigh" when they talk. That expulsion of a deep breath sounds sad or pitiful: "Poor me." It does little to assist you in exciting that audience about a new concept or challenging project. How do you stop? Same process. Just catch yourself.

Same too for pet phrases like, "you know"? or "right?" punctuating the end of every sentence. Record yourself, catch yourself and slowly stop using them.

Clarity

If you recorded yourself, listen, too, for clarity in your speech pattern. Do your words have endings? Can you hear the final letters, the "s," "ing," the "d," the "t"? If you cannot hear them, you may be slurring your words, making it difficult for the audience to decipher what you are saying.

Do you sound like "Goomominiznicetobespeak ineretoday?" Slow down and practice saying the ends of your words. There are exercises you can find like repeating, "She sells seashells by the seashore" or "Peter packed a peck of pickled peppers." Reciting and recording lines from poems or plays like "Friends, Romans, countrymen, lend me your ears" also may be helpful.

Emphasis

There is another aspect of speaking that is not related to the quality of your voice, pitch, pace, volume or clarity – it is about your use of emphasis.

To explain, read each of the following sentences, emphasizing the part of the sentence in **bold**:

I am delighted to be here today.

I *am* delighted to be here today.

I am *delighted* to be here today.

I am delighted to be *here* today.

I am delighted to be here *today*.

I am delighted / to be here today.

I am delighted / *to be here today*.

Remarkable, isn't it? By changing the emphasis, you can alter the meaning of the sentence. Think about this when you are practicing your talk. Decide whether there are key phrases or words that will enhance your meaning if you underline them with your voice.

In Summary

Presenting involves making decisions – before, during and after, not all in advance. In other words, when you are sending your message to the audience, what you do with your voice and speech pattern will assist you in assuring that your talk is both heard and intriguing. You have variables to play with: pacing, pausing, pitch, and volume. You may also want to think about your accent, your emphasis, your ability to project and whether there are sounds or words that distract and take away from your work.

Chapter 5
GETTING READY

"I keep six honest serving men
They taught me all I knew:
Their names are What and Why and When
And How and Where and Who."

Rudyard Kipling

In **Chapter 2** we recalled what is involved in the two-way communication process and its inherent problems. I am also encouraging you to become more aware of the implications of the physical aspects of presenting. Now let's look at the questions that you should ask once you have been selected or intend to speak. The answers to these questions can increase your professional image as well as your confidence, because you will be more in control. You will encounter fewer surprises. In addition, some of the answers should help you make decisions in advance about how and what you are going to say.

What are these questions? No surprise. They are the five "W's": "Who?" "What?" "Where?" "Why?" "When?" plus five more: "How?" "How many?" "How long?" "Who else?" and "Why me?" Although we will look at each one individually, every question is, in fact, one more thread that will help you form the tapestry of your talk. Let's examine each question to understand, first, what you want to learn by asking it, and second, what implications the answers have for your decision-making.

Why Me?

While this was the last question on the list, let's deal with
it first. It may sound silly, but this question seeks to
determine why you, and not someone else, were selected
to speak on this occasion. More often than not, the
answer to the question should build your confidence and
settle your nerves. The answer will probably be "You are
the best person to do it" or "You have been closest to the
project," which suggests that you "know your stuff," or
you will be told "You are good at presenting," which is
also nice to hear.

In the worst-case scenario, you may be told "No one else
wants to do it." But you can still be pleased because the
selector trusts you to give the talk.

Thus, the answer to "Why me?" should replace some
of the negative self-doubts with more positive notions
about your own competence.

How Long?

What you want to know is how much time the talk should take, including or in addition to any question time. The answer to the question will tell you that you have 10, 15 or 25 minutes. Pin it down further. Is it 15 minutes, plus 10 minutes for questions, a total of 25? Or is it 5 minutes with 10 minutes of questioning, a total of 15? Or is it 15 minutes with no questions? The answer may reveal that no one has thought about it yet. Press the issue and make a recommendation or get a decision. The length of time you have has critical implications for what you select for the content. Whether you have 15 or 25 minutes to talk about new product development will affect the amount of detail you can cover. Talk to the audience for 25 minutes, or will you need to involve them in some way?

Timing is important which is why earlier I encouraged you to wear a watch. How long you are allotted to speak amounts to a contract with the audience. When you ask, 'How long?' honor the answer. Ten minutes is 10 minutes, not 15. Twenty-five minutes is not 35 minutes.

Have you ever had a 10:30 appointment somewhere and been kept waiting until 11:00? Everyone responsible for that delay was apologetic, I am sure. But how did you feel? Annoyed? Angry? Impatient? Frustrated? Kicking yourself for being on time? Thinking about what else you might be doing besides reading old copies of *People* or *The Economist*? You elicit the same feelings in others when you speak longer than they expect you to.

Remember your responsibility to your audience? They have other meetings to attend and duties to perform. Of course, if you are invited to continue beyond the time, fine, but plan to say what has to be said in the time allotted. Worse yet is when you are one of a series of speakers, and each one runs three or four minutes longer than planned. Suppose you are scheduled to be the last speaker before lunch. Think about it. Will stomachs rumble and lunch be delayed because you started late, or will you find yourself being asked to cut out 10 minutes of your talk because the caterers are scheduled to serve at noon on the dot? Enough said! Watch the time! *You* watch it. Avoid letting someone else indicate that it is time to stop. It's your call.

Who Else?

What this question seeks to elicit is whether there will be any other people speaking. If so, who and about what and in what sequence? The answer again assists you in selecting your content. Be sure to request the time slot that you prefer, and if you learn that, yes, the CEO or Barack Obama or Beyoncé or some celebrity or expert in the field is speaking, you probably will prefer to be the speaker who precedes him or her.

So find out the sequence of speakers and decide where you want to be placed in relation to them. In addition to who they are, what they are expected to talk about is valuable information for you. For example, the Head of Finance might be talking about new cost-cutting measures, when the subject of your talk involves increased expenditure. In essence, you need to be aware whether the other speakers will have the same perspective that you have on a subject or opposing ones. Having this kind of knowledge in advance will help you include or exclude material or underline certain concepts. If possible, on the day, listen to the other speakers before you so you can incorporate, corroborate or disagree with their thoughts. It shows that you are a professional who listens.

How Many?

You ask this question to help establish your presentational style and perhaps the design of the talk. Typically, the larger the group, the more formal you may want to be. It is possible, but more difficult, to be casual and interactive with 250 people. By knowing how many will attend, you can think about any visuals or handouts you might need or be able to use for those numbers and to plan when and what you will design, print and/or copy. Maybe a flip chart or white board will be sufficient with five people. Perhaps slides, a film or a PowerPoint presentation will be necessary for 200 people. No need to take action yet. You are merely asking questions to collect data to help you make sensible decisions.

Where?

This question addresses both the location of the venue and the specific room you will be using for your talk. If you learn that the talk is in the conference room of the company where you work, that requires one kind of reconnaissance, but if you learn that the talk is to in the ballroom at a hotel in Hartford or Wellington, and you live in Denver, another type is required. If the event is off-site, and you must travel some distance, then you will need additional time for acclimatization and to ensure that you have the technology you need. A presentation in your own company's conference room should be less complicated, but you still should learn the room's strengths and limitations. **Chapter 10** addresses the importance of getting to know the venue – even if you are remote.

And if you're remote, substitute venue for technology: if you're a Zoom guru, and your talk is to be delivered over Teams, start learning the differences!

When?

As with the other questions, this one is seeking more than one piece of information. You want to know the date of your talk so that you can determine how much time you have to get organized – two weeks, a month, tomorrow at 10 a.m.

Based on what you hear, you may decide to say that you cannot do it. If you have been given too little time to prepare what you know constitutes a professional talk, you may want to decline. Your good name is at stake. Sometimes you can influence someone else's decision. Negotiate. "Tuesday is not possible, but Thursday is," you might say. Make choices about the timing that are better for you, if possible. Naturally, if you are asked to speak at a board meeting that is scheduled for the third Thursday of every month, you will probably have no choice. But when you have options that afford you the opportunity to better prepare, take them.

Are you being asked to speak right after lunch? Do you want to? Analyze your own working style. Do you concentrate better in the morning? Are you a morning person, or are you more alert at 3:00 p.m.?

The answer to "When?" also may have implications for design. Do you think that the mood of the audience on Tuesday morning after a long weekend will be the same as on a Friday afternoon? You know how you feel in such circumstances. Will you be speaking at the same time as a World Cup broadcast, or an All-Ireland Hurling Final, or the final heats of the 5,000 meters at the Olympics, or a national election, or the Academy Awards? Will the dead of winter or the brilliance of a summer day affect the group? As soon as you know the "When?" decide what may interfere with your talk being received or what aspect of the timing provides an opportunity to reinforce your message.

Who?

Because of the emphasis on audience throughout this book, you know that this is a key question. Remember the two-way communication process? The answer to "Who?" assists you in understanding more about the receivers of your message and, therefore, what kind of codes you should select for them. The answer to the earlier question "How many?" gives you the number in attendance. Now you want more specific information, if at all possible, about those unique individuals.

On one level, a simple demographic breakdown helps. What is the sex, age, education, nationality, and work experience of the audience? Is English their first language? What are their job titles? What types of organizations or departments are they working in? Or what kinds of organizations do they belong to or represent – private, non-profit, large, small, retail, or financial? This information is important whether the talk is being delivered within your own organization or at a teleconference. Naturally, you will be more familiar with your own colleagues, but, even so, remember to ask who is going to be there: The Marketing Director? The Head of R&D? All the PAs? The secretarial staff? Only the accountants?

With some groups, find out, if you can, some of the internal politics. Who has just been promoted? Who was bypassed? Who is counting the days to retirement? Who must attend the meeting but does not want to? Who might be hostile? Who is looking for a promotion? In other words, the more you know about the group, the more accurately you will be able to select the appropriate data, examples and anecdotes for your talk, and you will be able to eliminate what you believe is known by all. For example, if everyone in the audience has been in the industry or working in the company for five years or more, you may only need to provide a cursory review of the history of the new product line. If there are new members of staff present, you may have to devote more time explaining the background. Or suppose your talk is primarily about findings from some market research. It is helpful to know your audience's comfort level with certain terms and concepts. If they are unfamiliar with the subject, you may need to include more basic information.

What you are doing is seeking data to balance what your audience already knows with what it needs to learn, to enable you to make educated decisions about the audience's knowledge of your topic. You also will be developing a sense of their level of interest. If you discover that everyone has been ordered to attend the meeting, you may have a different motivational task than if you learn that they all chose to attend.

Why all the demographic stuff if you know their job titles? As you will see in **Chapter 6**, an effective talk is filled with real-life examples, images and anecdotes. Therefore, the more you know about the audience, the more accurate you can be in selecting these stories. Given what you know about a group's age, sex, job titles, nationality, you will be in a better position to decide whether you can refer to Ice-T, Madonna, Maureen O'Hara, BMWs, Paris fashions, Grunge, Brad Pitt, Marketshare, Nelson Mandela, a scrum, base hit, rugby, soccer, knitting or cooking. Will they know to what or to whom you referring when you make such allusions? Are the examples ancient history or too obtuse?

What?

This question concerns the content of your talk. When you pose it, the answer should clarify the theme, the subject matter. Of course, the scope or depth of the talk will be affected by the amount of time you have. For example, are you supposed to discuss the marketing plan for all the company's products, or the plan for one product in the line? Or are you supposed to discuss one aspect of the plan for a particular product? If you learn that you are to explain a new policy, are you expected to include the rationale for the policy as well as the implementation, or are you only being asked to explain the content of the policy itself? In other words, the question "What?" sets the parameters of the talk. Until you have a complete answer to this question, though, your talk may have little impact or none at all.

Why?

This question goes beyond the content. You ask it to determine the purpose of the talk. Suppose the answer to your "What?" question was to talk about a new attendance policy. The next question, "Why?", seeks to determine a rationale for the audience's knowing about the policy. In other words, you must articulate what you want them to do as a result of what you are telling them. You are in search of the "hook."

Do you want them to understand the new policy to avoid confusion? Do you want them simply to understand that there is a new policy? Do you want them to understand that there are grave implications for violating the policy? Do you want them to understand those implications? Do you want them to be at ease with the change of policy? Are you showing how the new policy is similar to the old one? Do you want them to see the benefits of the policy? Do you want to tell them about the new policy so that they will be more accepting of it because they have had information shared with them? Are they going to vote on the new policy? Is there any debate, or is it a *fait accompli*?

The answers to "What?" and "Why?" will ensure that you and the audience know exactly the point of your talk. They may not like what they hear, but if you have prepared well, they will understand what the subject was and why it is important for them to hear it.

How?

This question seeks to determine the best method for organizing your talk. Does the person who nominated you already have a plan in mind? Is it to be a panel discussion? Would a question and answer approach be better? Are you being asked to talk for 20 minutes? Are you supposed to read a paper for 35 minutes? Some plans may already be in place, but you may decide, given the answers you have to the "What?" "Why?" and "Who?", that the initial design needs modifying. It may be boring or too structured, too interactive or too casual. Each one of these preceding questions is separate yet interrelated. Talking for 45 minutes to 100 senior managers who are used to taking charge may not work. You have to ponder what will. And, if you're speaking virtually, remember Zoom fatigue.

Suppose you discover that your job is to design a presentation for 15 junior staff. You want to involve them in a group discussion, but you also know that three of their supervisors will be present, thus making for a potentially threatening atmosphere, which may affect the participants' willingness to speak out. Alternatively, you might have to figure out how to structure what you say to keep 30 people, including 25 engineers and five HR folks engaged in a talk on performance appraisal that is scheduled for 2:30 on Thursday. The solutions are up to you and your creativity.

In Summary

As you gather the information based on the answers to the five "W"s – plus the additional five questions of "How?" "How many?" "How long?" "Who else?" and "Why?" you are making content decisions about what to include and exclude and how to say it.

In the process, you may accept all the givens or assert your own views, based on your awareness of possible human conflicts or venue limitations. You may be negotiating for five or 10 minutes more or less, or for a room that is bigger or smaller, or perhaps recommending that the talk be given separately to two groups rather than one because of your conviction that the message can be coded and received more accurately doing it that way. Perhaps two meetings, with breakouts on Zoom, would work. You are in a better position to decide what you may want the participants to do and what you will do. By asking key questions and making any recommendations for change based on the answers, you should be armed with valuable information for the next phase of the process, the actual preparation of your speech.

Chapter 6
PREPARING YOUR SPEECH

"To communicate, put your thoughts in order; give them
a purpose; use them to persuade, to instruct, to
discover, to seduce."

William Safire, columnist, The *New York Times*

"A speech is a solemn responsibility. The man who
makes a bad 30-minute speech to 200 people wastes
only a half-hour of his time. But he wastes 100 hours of
the audience's time – more than four days – which
should be a hanging offense."

Jenkin Lloyd Jones, American writer

Let's look at your speech from three perspectives: first
selecting data to support your message or purpose;
second, how best to organize it; and third, some of your
actual word choices.

Once you have asked and received answers to the
questions listed in **Chapter 5**, it is time to collect the
data that you will need for the talk itself to make your
point or points clearly, accurately and convincingly. It
may require interviewing, researching or analyzing. And
rest assured, you will accumulate more information than
you need. Unfortunately, having gathered that precious
data, some speakers are reluctant to let go, so they

include all of it in the finished product. The result is information overload, or "waffle." Instead, with the precise subject and purpose in mind, sift through the material you have, eliminating what may be tangential or charming but irrelevant for your objective.

Select only what establishes the context and supports your arguments for the position you are espousing. If you have material on the construction of the Omaha plant, the subject, and you have data on the one in Nashville, be brave and file the Nashville information for a future talk – unless it makes your point about Omaha.

How you initially organize your thoughts is up to you. Some folks immediately start designing slides. Some people make lists of bullet points or write random notions. Others prefer to make an outline. Still others write headings and group relevant ideas under each one. I encourage reflecting and writing. Putting your thoughts together for a talk is the same as organizing your ideas for a written report; select whatever method works well for you. What is important is that you go through the thinking, refining and narrowing process to create a preliminary structure.

Remember you are constrained by the necessity of relying on your verbal clarity. There is no next paragraph or appendix for the audience to read, or to reread for that matter. You are also constrained by the time you have available to you to discuss your subject. Look at your material and prepare a draft, selecting only what keeps you on target.

Having asked all the preparatory questions, you should have a good idea about the audience's level of knowledge about your topic as well as their frame of reference, so decide what technical terms you need to use or define and how much background is essential. Suppose you plan to discuss the results of a recent safety audit. If your preliminary questioning establishes that your audience already knows about the audit, you may only want to devote a few sentences to the rationale for the audit and description of the auditors. You can focus on the findings and the subsequent implications and/or recommendations.

Of course, it is more difficult to gauge what is essential to include in a talk when you have a diverse group coming from different departments or backgrounds, or from the public. What may be old hat to financial people may be new to those in R&D or *vice versa*. Their perspectives on issues may be varied; seek a balance that meets the needs of both groups. Sometimes the best way is to acknowledge orally the degree of diversity. This could be as simple as, "Although most of you are familiar with, some of you may not, so let me clarify … ."

You know what the subject is and why you are talking about it. You have the essential material and have eliminated the nonessentials. Keeping the audience foremost in your mind, you can anticipate some of the questions or arguments about the subject matter. Salespeople sometimes call this process "overcoming objections." To prepare for possible challenges, think through the topic examining it from the audience's perspective. Then, build *their* arguments and objections into your speech. You might say, for example, "Some of you may be wondering why we need a new policy at all, when the previous policy ..." and then proceed to explain why; or you might indicate that you anticipate that "Some of you may have questions, please hold them 'til later."

The Structure

So far, you have asked, gathered, included, excluded, added, and deleted possible key ideas and identified those that are vital to making your position clear. It is time to refine the initial structure of the speech and to organize the material within it. The specific questions that I recommended you ask in preparation came as no surprise to you. This next step should be familiar to you as well. Every talk needs a beginning, middle and an end: an introduction, body and conclusion. We all know that, but what is important is what you want to accomplish in each of the sections.

The beginning of the talk is designed to grab or "hook" the audience's attention, to focus their thoughts on you and on what you are saying. It is the part of the speech in which you state the objectives of the talk, sometimes including its length and the approach that you plan to use. "During the next 20 minutes," you might say, "we will review point by point the __." You also might include the limitations; that is, you might explain what you are not going to talk about, so you establish expectations: "I will only be talking about __, not __."

The middle of the talk is where you state your points, facts, arguments, and/or rationales. Here is the opportunity to elaborate on each of those arguments or ideas. It is the heart of the speech and includes the supporting data you have amassed to make your argument.

At the end of the talk, you can restate your original objective and request that they take some action based on what you have said or recommended. Suppose you stated in the beginning that the objective of the talk was to give X number of reasons why Ireland is an ideal tourist destination. The middle would have elaborated on all those arguments. Then, in the closing, you restate your objective and tell the audience what you want them to do. If they are potential tourists, you may ask them to: visit, tell their relatives, read a book, consider a bus tour, change their plans or bring their golf clubs. If they are folks in the hospitality industry, you may ask them to consider altering their traditional marketing plans. You state what it is that you want from them. Thus, they leave the room with that message firmly in their minds.

The Beginning

Even though I encourage you to write your opening last, let's talk about it first. If part of the intent of your talk's beginning is to be motivational and to have people focus on you and your words, let's look at some of the methods for coaxing people to take their overwhelmed minds off their other concerns and responsibilities and listen to you. How can you "hook" them?

The straightforward approach is to simply state your objective: "Smoking is considered a health hazard, and today we will review the current medical findings." Fine.

Consider other choices for your opening remarks that you may find useful. You may want to begin with a quotation, "George Lucas said ..." or "John Kennedy is quoted as saying ... ." Or you may choose to tell a relevant story or anecdote: "A few years ago ..." or "The last time I spoke in ..." or "There is a wonderful story that ... ."

Another option is to establish rapport by telling an appropriate joke – if you are a good joke-teller. Jokes though, can be worrisome, because no matter how witty you are, the audience may not be amused. If you are not feeling confident to begin with, and your audience fails to laugh, then the lack of reaction may make you feel more uncomfortable.

Besides stories, jokes and quotations, another approach is to begin a talk with a question: "Do you ...?" or "Have you ...?" or "How many of you ...?" From my experience asking for a show of hands is safer than asking a specific question. Raising hands is a silent, group action. Asking for a show of hands avoids people calling out, which you may have to deal with, and individual answers may eat into your limited time. You also risk not getting the feedback you think you are going to get. Questioning is a wonderful technique; just anticipate what might happen.

Yet another opening is to use a statistic or a shocking fact. A now famous opener was used by a Professor of Medicine who gazed out at his first-year students and asked them to look first to their right and then to their left, "Because," he said, "only one out of the three of you will be sitting here on the first day of term next year." You can be certain that he got their attention!

Some people use dramatic approaches; they make strange noises, throw objects, wear shocking clothing, burst balloons, but that kind of novelty works for some speakers, not all. Like asking questions, unless you are prepared, the downside risk of that kind of theatricality is that the audience may remember the balloons or the shocking clothing but be unable to recall the content of the talk that followed.

In other words, you have a variety of options to choose from. Those opening lines are limited only by your imagination, so you may want to experiment with different styles to determine what works for you.

The Middle

As you structure the middle of your talk, remember what we said earlier about inattentiveness or distraction being a barrier to effective communication. To help people stay focused, design your presentation by repeating key words, ideas or phrases. Commercials illustrate this point. New ideas and behaviors are fragile, which is why it takes time for a new speaker to eliminate the "em" sound between sentences. In the same way, until the idea is ingrained, the listener may forget, so repeat your key points. Remember how you were taught vocabulary as a youngster or when you were learning another language? Repetition. Repetition. Repetition.

As we said, the heart of the matter is the middle. It is in this section of your speech that you explain or expand on the issues that you indicated you were going to discuss. Suppose, as we said earlier, that you have been asked to talk about why Ireland is an ideal tourist destination, and you have told the audience in the beginning that there are 10 reasons. In the body of the talk, you develop each one of the 10. Do your best to sequence those 10 items to aid retention.

Suppose you have a process to describe or the stages or phases of a plan to explain – "The new recruiting process has five steps." In the middle of the talk, you clarify or justify each of the five steps sequentially. Or you may be giving a talk in which you are arguing for and against something – the pros and cons, for example, of investing in a new technology. In this instance, you may organize the middle by discussing all five positives first followed by the five negatives, or you may present one pro and then one con, then the next pro and the next con, and so on. Regardless of the approach you choose, try to create a logical sequence. If you offer three pros, two cons, then the final two pros and last three cons, it may be difficult for the audience to follow your thinking. Keep it as clear as you can.

Or suppose you have five arguments to support a recommendation for investing in a particular technology.

Decide in what order to put each of the five. In other words, which is number one, and which recommendations are numbers two, three, four and five? Establish the sequence rather than having a random order, or one based on your data collection. Do you want the most important reason first? Do you want it last? Your decision affects where the least important reason goes, first or last. Which arguments do you want in the middle of your list? In what order? Why? Again, we remember beginnings and endings better than the middle of sequences.

If the subject of your talk is your five-year-plan, the natural sequence might be chronological – past to present to future: what was, what is, and what might or could be. Or do you prefer to work in the opposite direction, future to past? When you establish your sequence, keep in mind that the audience is being asked to recall information primarily aurally. So, not having a report to reread, numbered lists and sequenced information assist them in following and retaining your thoughts.

Numbering, while convenient, is not always possible or appropriate. Suppose you are charged with explaining a theoretical construct. Theory is abstract and may be difficult to comprehend. so give the audience an example of the theory at work or an example of its application.

Remember Maslow's Hierarchy of Needs? It is invariably pictured as a pyramid, a simple device that helps you visualize the concept. The top of the pyramid is usually labeled self-actualization. But what does that mean? You cannot hold self-actualization or touch it. So, if you think back to the first time you met that particular pyramid, either the author or the instructor gave you examples of what self-actualization means to real people, or the speaker asked what the words meant to you.

The lesson here is: when dealing with an abstract concept, do your best to create a visual image or example. You can talk about the location of diverse functions of the human brain, or you can show a picture of the areas. You can discuss the concept of strategic planning, but it helps to give examples. You can discuss the changes in IT, but offer the audience an image, application, example or analogy. Imagine trying to persuade tourists to visit Ireland without showing them actual pictures of the beauty spots?

Suppose your talk is about the layout of a new structure, you might organize your talk spatially, moving from the description of the left side to the right, or from the top to the bottom or from the bottom to the top.

What I am encouraging you to do is to plan your talk in a way that enables the audience to stay focused because you are using verbal logic. Again, no rules. A talk could be sequenced to discuss macro issues and then micro ones. Challenges and opportunities? If the subject is geographical, maybe you want to speak in terms of East to West or West to East or North to South or the reverse or in terms of the size of the market.

If none of these approaches fits the subject, then look for other methods of organizing the data. But do find one. Could it be in terms of strengths and weaknesses? In terms of similarities and differences? Could you raise several questions and then answer each one in turn?

Numbering is always useful. It's easy to follow and to take notes, to say nothing of the fact that you have fingers to use. If you use numbers, do so consistently. If you say that you have five points and proceed to discuss numbers one, and two and then say "number four is ..." inadvertently forgetting to say the number three, members of the audience may check with their neighbors to find out what happened to number three. They may be talking to each other, or on the chat screen reflecting on you or on their error, and are no longer listening.

Another mechanism for creating internal structure and aiding retention is by using memory aids or mnemonics. As you organize your thoughts, you may discover that certain key words or ideas stand out. When you write them down, note the first letter of each word. Can you make a new word or acronym from those letters that will help the audience remember your key ideas? For example, "Today we are examining a DREAM." You then explain that the letter D stands for development, R for reason and so on, with each letter representing one of the points that you are making.

Are you familiar with AIDA in selling? Each letter stands for a key concept – attention, interest, desire, action. ABC is another: Always Be Closing. The objective of using the mnemonic is to help the listener remember. As usual, there is a *caveat*: be careful that your mnemonic is not too long; for example, ENVIRONMENT, E = energy, N = nature, V = vegetation, etc. The audience may only remember the acronym and not what the letters stand for.

You know what you are saying, and why you are saying it. You have identified the data you are using to substantiate your arguments and have eliminated certain tangential or unnecessary material. You have structured the middle.

Now go back and reflect on what you want to include in the opening, the part that is designed to motivate the audience to listen and for you to state your objectives. As we said earlier, you may tell them what you are not including. In research, that is often called the "limitations of the study." What that means is that you are telling the audience precisely what the parameters are and letting them know what they should not expect to hear. In that way, you narrow their focus to only the points that you plan to talk about.

For example, suppose you are speaking about your organization's current appraisal system. You may opt to indicate that you are speaking only about the system for the support staff, not the one for the technical staff, or you may indicate that you are speaking only about the system that has been in place for the past three years, not the older one. Or if your talk is about 10 reasons for visiting Ireland, you may say that this presentation is limited to the Spring and Summer, or for the visitor who is under 35 or for families with teenage children. In that way, you clarify what you are going to include.

The Closing

Finally, let's look at closing lines. Speeches are like sandwiches. One slice of bread is the opening, the other is the closing, with the "meat" in the middle. So, to put the final slice of bread on, I recommend that you use what you chose for your opening. For example, suppose you chose to start the talk with a quotation from George Lucas or John F. Kennedy, you might end it with the same one or a different one by Steven Spielberg and another president. Suppose you began by asking a question; you might end with the answer to the opening question, or by restating the original one or asking yet another. If you started with a story, end with a story. Did you start with a statistic? Then close with one.

You plan this in advance. To reiterate, because we remember beginnings and endings better than the middles, take the time to find an effective way to grab their attention at the outset and to remind them at the end what you told them and what you want from them. This is the organization of the talk: a beginning with a solid appropriate attention-getting device, a statement of the objectives, explanation of the limitations followed by a middle that is logically sequenced, then a closing that restates your objectives – the "What?" and ""Why?" you were talking about the subject. You have outlined the talk. It is a strong skeleton, and now you flesh it out with words and examples. How do you do that?

Specificity

Be specific, whenever possible. If you choose words like "huge," "tremendous," "great," "wonderful," "vast," "costly," "enormous," or "awesome," the audience has no frame of reference. Is it as "vast" as Central Park or the Sahara Desert? In other words, my idea of what signifies "huge" may be different from yours. What is "costly" to me may be a pittance to you. Is a "stack" of paper a foot high or an inch deep? Therefore, use specifics: 15%, $4, next Tuesday, what improvements exactly. The more specific you can be, the less your audience will suffer from "waffle." Think of all the trivia games that proliferate because of our ability to retain specifics. How did James Bond take his martini: "Shaken, not __"? Invariably in workshops when I ask participants what they remember of their colleagues' talks, the answers are specifics, images, and facts.

Analogies

Another useful tool to aid retention is to make analogies or to use examples that bring your subject to life. Is the budget equivalent to the national debt? Were the hailstones the size of golf balls? Was the office so crowded it looked like Starbuck's on a Monday morning? Were the people so delighted they looked like Patrick Mahomes after he had completed another touchdown pass? Was it so hot that you could cook eggs on the road? In other words, whenever possible, provide verbal images, specifics or analogies.

Word Choice

It is impossible to review every word or phrase you might have in a talk; however, let's examine some of the frequently selected words and phrases that you might want to avoid in the same way I encourage you to eliminate certain gestures or other movements that detract from your presentation.

Let's dispense with one group quickly. Those are words or phrases that may be inappropriate, clever or sarcastic; remarks that are demeaning, insulting or stereotyping and touch on sex, job, age, religion, ethnic background, politics and disability. You know the list; while preparing, double-check that you have not slipped something into your talk by mistake. It is easy to offend, and when you do, you risk alienating someone who may be a member of a particular group or related to someone who is or who may have strong feelings on the subject.

When you refer to women as "girls" or managers as "he" or describe "over 50s" as sedentary, you risk offending. Let the audience make the snide comment about a recent political *faux pas* in some country; don't you do it. An inappropriate reference may cost you the attention and members of the audience. They may focus on the remark, think about it and either lose the flow of the talk or, worse yet, resent you for articulating values that are incompatible with their own. It is an expensive error. Let's be clear that what I am referring to is your choice of examples or asides. The subject matter itself may be difficult for some people to take, such as, layoffs. Just be careful of inadvertent insults.

Be mindful, too, when you select your supporting data, of saying something that is wrong, inaccurate, illegal or unethical. Suppose, for example, you cite references to events that occurred in 2018 when, in fact, they occurred in 2009. Someone in the audience who is aware of the error may see a crack in your credibility. You will have a difficult time regaining their trust. If one statistic is wrong, will there be others? As you frequently hear on crime shows when witnesses are interrogated on the stand, "If you were lying then, are you lying now?"

When you run through your talk, evaluate your specific word choices. And look for the words we mentioned earlier that are annoying or distracting. They are single words or phrases like "OK," "well," "right," "as you know," "at this stage," or "as such." There's nothing wrong with any of them but be careful that your pet phrase isn't sprinkled throughout without realizing you are doing it. Such words and phrases only constitute a problem when they are used with such frequency that the audience notices them and begins to count. For example, if you say "OK" at the end of every sentence or every time you click the remote, the audience may begin to keep track. As we said, notice if you repeat certain expressions, because you risk the audience's becoming distracted and focusing on them, rather than on your talk. So, catch yourself, if you are in the habit of starting a sentence with "Well" or "Right"! Think of the wasted effort. All that time you devoted to finding the right opening words and then undermining your creativity with "Well"! How do you stop? Remember you cure yourself the same way that you stop other habits: catch yourself doing it and then gradually decrease the frequency.

Another *caveat* about phrases: watch out for self-deprecating ones: "I hope that I did not bore you" or "I am just going to talk about …" or "I am only going to take a few minutes," or, when you close, "Well, that's it!" After all your work, organizing, structuring, looking for examples and analogies, what are you apologizing for? You may think the phrases or words, like "only" and "just" are endearing or humble. In fact, they may seem insincere.

The reality is that you worked hard to create an organized, clear presentation and should be proud of your effort. Let there be no misunderstanding, the phrase "I am just going to talk about …" is different from telling a story on yourself, about a mistake you made or about weight that you have gained over the holidays. Revealing a foible can be charming and may help establish rapport. But please make no apologies for your hard work on behalf of the audience.

Another specific sentence that you might want to avoid using is: "Today I am going to talk about … ." Eliminate that phrase and plunge right into the talk. For example, instead of "I am going to talk about the importance of increasing our __," try "Increasing our __ is important." It is more direct.

While we are at it, think, too, about which pronoun you want to use. While it may be a small point, do you want to use "I" or "we"? As you know, "I" separates; "we" joins. If you believe that your message will be received better with "we," by all means, use it.

There are two additional minor points: one about "finally;" the other is about "Thank you." "Finally" or "In conclusion" should be said only once, when your talk is almost over. With that phrase, you are signaling to the audience that you are almost finished. You may have noticed that many speakers say "finally," keep on talking and add "And, my last point is ...," keep on talking and say, "So, in summary ..." keep on talking and say, "Therefore, to conclude ... ." Please conclude your talk once.

And then there is "Thank you." As you know, the objective of the final sentence in your talk is to reinforce your main points, underline your message or call to action, so avoid letting your "Thank you" slide into the final words. Say your final sentence – then pause. Like the final notes of a piece of music, there is a moment of silence which is usually followed by a round of applause, or some key person will thank you on behalf of those present. They are saying "Thank you" to you by clapping. You, however, thank them for their expression of gratitude, be it applause or kind words. Why all the fuss about such a simple point? It is a pity to hear a well-thought-out final thought lost by closing amenities. So, say what you have to say, pause or stop, and then acknowledge their reaction. You have earned it!

In Summary

Having asked your preliminary questions, assembled the data, bearing your purpose and audience in mind. Organize your talk into three sections: beginning, middle and end and sequence the middle to aid retention. Both the beginning and the end state your message and are designed to help focus attention on you and your words.

Once you have a draft, find ways to bring in analogies and specifics that are accurate and appropriate. Then it is time to rehearse to increase your comfort level and check the timing, while noting any extraneous words and remarks that, like inappropriate body language, detract from your key ideas.

Chapter 7
USING NOTES

"William Graham spoke without a note, and almost without a point."
Winston Churchill

Now that you have thought through and drafted your presentation, it is time to make yet another decision. This one is about using notes. This chapter underlines the importance of having prompts or reminders. We will not be discussing electronic options, such as teleprompters.

You may have written the talk in longhand, typed and printed it or jotted notes on paper or cards or slides to speak extemporaneously. Or, you may have decided to memorize it.

Because I wrote about my fiasco years ago, when I froze and forgot everything, then you know that I advise against relying solely on your memory. The downside risk is enormous. If anything goes wrong, that distracts, that causes you to lose your concentration, or that causes you to become anxious, then the worst can happen. Your doubts will be realized, and you, too, may forget it all. If you ask other people, you will discover that memory lapses happen at one time or another to every speaker. It is possible to look at the audience and panic or to have a major disruption and lose focus, or to be asked a question in mid-stream and to lose your place. Not to worry; it rarely happens. But it might; so, unless you have a masochistic need to experience that kind of discomfort, use or have notes of some kind. By the way, having notes or cue cards humanizes you in the eyes of the audience and makes you more credible.

Reading *versus* Using Notes

Before looking more closely at what you write down for notes, let's consider reading a speech. You see that approach at professional conferences where presenters "deliver a paper." Reading papers is not about establishing rapport; it is virtually impossible to establish any eye contact, to weigh reactions and to alter pace, pitch, volume or content based on what you are experiencing. Try reading this page as if there were an audience in front of you. Notice that when you look up from the page, to look at the audience, it is easy to lose your place.

Reading a paper also makes you more dependent on a lectern, because you need to put the sheets or laptop on something. If you hold pages in your hands, they can become problematic, particularly as you read near the bottom or turn them. In addition, it's noisy, and, if there is a microphone, everyone may hear the crackle. If you do decide to read your report, be sure to use good quality paper and not pages torn from a yellow legal pad. You have seen that. If you do, you risk giving the impression that you wrote the talk hurriedly or on the way over to the meeting. The audience should know you have invested time in them.

Instead of reading, some presenters use their slides as prompts or notes. Using slides as prompts raises a crucial question. Ask yourself whether the visuals were designed for you or for the audience. We have all seen and sat through talks in which the PowerPoint is the speaker's notes. They were designed to aid the speaker. You recognize them because the information is usually random, disjointed or wordy.

Using your slides as notes may cause you to have too many slides or leave you without notes until you power-on the computer. And technology, as miraculous as it is, is technology! In one workshop, a participant indicated that they now bring three laptops to back each other up because, in previous presentations, two had failed. In other words, strike a balance that works for you. You want to have some sort of cue cards should your emotions or events distract you. Some folks use a folded sheet of paper with key points; others have notes separately on the computer; still others use their phones.

This last option is the least desirable. The audience identifies with how we all use our phones – checking texts? And it narrows your focus. If you do use your phone, consider telling your audience that it has your notes on it.

For years I have opted for old-fashioned lined cards. Why cards? Paper, as noted previously, is awkward and noisy; 3" x 5" or 4" x 6" cards are sturdier. They fit easily in my hand, and in a pocket, so I can carry and practice with them. And unless I shuffle them, they are noise-free.

Using Note Cards

What do you put on the cards? First, you write on only one side of the card, and number them in sequence, in case they become disordered. Write in letters large enough to enable you to see what you have written if you are holding them at arm's length. On each card, you might write one of your key ideas, justifications or rationales. After the key idea, write the word or phrases sufficient to remind you of the examples that you plan to use to bring that idea to life.

4. The climate of Ireland
   - maritime
   - temperate
   - changeable

If you keep only one idea on a card, all you need to do is add one or delete one if you are modifying the talk and giving it again. No need to retype the whole speech or squeeze in your ideas on the margin of the paper.

You may want one card devoted to the introduction completely written out. Doing that is extra insurance at the beginning when you are most likely to be more unsettled and might want the additional support.

In addition to your cards with the key ideas, you may reproduce simple visuals onto your cards, so that you will not have to turn your back to the audience, if you can't see them on a laptop in front of you.

And, if you are using a film clip, be sure to stand back and to the side so your audience can see it.

Practicing with Notes

Using cards for the first time may feel awkward, so practice using them. Notice how they allow you to be more mobile. As we said, sheets of paper or a laptop require you to be near the lectern, which is not always desirable. The only support the cards need is from your hands, so you have more freedom. In addition, the cards give you something to do with your hands, thus resolving the issue of those extra appendages that appeared when you walked to the front. You can hold your hands in such a way that a quick glance down at your notes and then back up again to the audience is all you need to continue. Thus, you break your eye contact with the audience only briefly.

Again, if this is a new technique for you, it takes time to adjust to using cards. A few minor points, as you practice: if you have the habit of holding your hands together as you speak, avoid holding the cards that way.

One hand could hold the pack, and the other may hold the card that you are referring to. Then move it to the bottom when you are finished with it. And the second recommendation: avoid fidgeting with the cards, turning them around, rolling, twisting or tapping with them. If you do, then your notes themselves become a distraction. And, when you have finished with card number one or two, please do not throw the finished cue card on the nearest table as if you are eager to be rid of it. Hold onto them all – with pride. They represent hours of work reduced to a pack of 3" x 5" cards.

In Summary

As you become more comfortable working with notes, you may find them reassuring, too. With your key words written down, you eliminate the fear of blanking out; you have what you are going to say. If you become distracted by someone or something, notes can bring you back on track by reminding you where you left off and where you still need to go.

Chapter 8
USING VISUALS AND HANDOUTS

"Visuals act as punctuation points in your presentation. They offer relief to the audience and make the audience's commitment a series of short decisions to stay tuned instead of one long, unattractive obligation."

Ed Brenner, photographer and publisher

"A picture may instantly present what a book could set forth only in 100 pages."

Ivan Turgenev

We have referred to visuals several times. This chapter is dedicated to them because they warrant more than a passing reference. Visuals are used to assist the audience in retaining and understanding information. When we see and hear about something at the same time, it stays in our minds. For example, you can describe your office verbally to an audience, by simultaneously showing a picture as you are talking, so your audience has a better sense of what you want them to understand. You can talk about Daniel Day-Lewis' portrayal of Christy Brown or Lincoln, or you can show a photograph as you speak. The impact is different. That is why you use visuals, which can be words, pictures, films, graphs, charts or props. Let's consider them separately, along with handouts.

Once your talk is outlined, and your key points and supporting examples for each thought through, review your speech and determine where a visual would clarify a point or reinforce your words, and what kind of visual would accomplish that best. Remember you do not use graphics because you think every talk requires them. You use them because they make a difference.

Often a presentation is a follow-up to a study or report, so speakers use the report itself as the basis for the talk. Unfortunately, in some cases, the visuals are actual copies of pages taken out of the report, either from the appendix or from the findings. The problem is that that is what the visuals look like – pages from a written report, small font, page numbers and all.

As you know, written documents are different from talks, and as we said, one difference is that reports can be read and reread over time by an individual in isolation. Such material can be read in sections, filed, and picked up again. Because the reader can pore over it at leisure, a table or a chart in a report can be more detailed and have smaller print than one in a talk. An audience for a talk does not have that luxury. In essence, you cannot necessarily use a visual designed for another medium. To repeat: decide what the audience needs to see to help them retain or understand information and how you want them to see it. Consider your choice of colors too. Are your pie charts too pastel? Do you need more contrast?

Before examining what else an effective visual looks like, determine what kind of visuals, if any, would be appropriate. To help you, factor in the number of people present. Do you want them to have a handout at the end when they leave? Or would it be better for them to have some written material before you start? Have you no need at all for videos, handouts, or PowerPoint slides because you feel that writing on a white board is better? Will a flipchart be sufficient? A PDF or a shared screen? Make your decisions based on considerations such as: the degree of formality, purpose of the talk, nature of the topic, size of the room, live or remote, and number of people. Producing videos may be expensive and time-consuming, while creating your own visual clarification or reinforcements with a white board or flip chart may be more immediate and casual. You can also opt to "pre-flip" or write on the board in advance.

Let's suppose you have decided to use PowerPoint and want one slide with the title of your talk and one for each of your key points. In addition, you might include one or two with charts or graphs to demonstrate a particular trend that supports your argument, perhaps a picture of the product you are discussing, and a map indicating some demographic data.

When you design these graphics, what should you take into consideration? You know all these answers. First, any slide primarily devoted to words should be kept simple and use a font that is large enough and dark enough against the background for everyone in the room to see. Leave sufficient "white space" around the margins and between the points, so that the slide is uncluttered and easy to read from anywhere in the room or on-screen at a virtual meeting. Avoid complete sentences; instead, use phrases or bullet points. Check that the language of each point is consistent.

Look at this:

```
The purpose of the research was to:
• determine the ...
• assess the ...
• conclusions about the ...
```

Notice that this speaker begins each of the first two points with a verb, "determine" and "assess," and the third point with a noun, "conclusions." For consistency (which aids clarity), the third item in the list should also be a verb: "conclude." Alternatively, the first two points could become nouns, "determination" and "assessment." If you choose nouns, then you also would have to change the stem to: "The purpose of the research was to make ... ." This consistency makes it easier for the audience to follow. Be sure, too, that the points on your graphic are lined up one under each other, not two spaces to the left:

```
    • determine the ...
•   assess the ...
    • conclude that ...
    • recommend that ...
```

Such carelessness distracts your audience. Inconsistent use of upper and lower case is equally annoying:

- Determine the ...
- assess the ...
- Conclude that ...

Remember to make the time to proofread for typographical errors: "invoolment," "accomodation," "liason," missing or misplaced apostrophes. A typo signals to the audience that you are inattentive to detail – especially a typo referring to the audience. I recently saw a speaker who presented to members of the professional body, Chartered Accountants Ireland. The opening slide referred to "Charted Accounts Ireland." Some participants may wonder why you did not check on these details and may consider your data suspect as well. If the audience allows that possibility to creep into their minds, your credibility may be questioned. If you are under time constraints, better not use visuals than have any that are flawed.

Besides ensuring that you have a good layout, consistent language and no typos, title or label the slide, particularly charts and graphs. Too often, speakers spend time creating an excellent visual representation and then forget to label it. Bear in mind that people can be distracted by a noise or by someone coming into the room late, or at home – a puppy. What a pity to have an exquisitely designed pie chart on the screen with percentages carefully explaining each segment, but the audience will not know what the figures represent if there is no title. So, label your graphics, especially if you are showing more than one chart.

Suppose you are using a graph to reflect a trend. It, too, needs to be labeled and titled. You may find that the audience follows you better if you have one showing the basic data, the axis, then build on it with another showing the changes. Help the audience grasp the information bit by bit and assist them by providing the information systematically.

To highlight a point in your visual, you may want to put an arrow next to a critical bar on the graph or a circle around a key intersection. During the presentation you may use your finger or a pointer, remembering never directing it at the audience. Often laser pointers look like fireflies flitting around the screen, so tell them where you want them to focus: "If you look at the last column on the right", or "Look at the top of the screen." Otherwise, they will be taking in the information as they choose, rather than as you wish them to.

Also, try to create logical sequences on your visuals, just as you did for the body of the talk. Numbers and years need careful organizing. Stay chronological, if you can: 2010-2011, 2011-2012 not 2013-2014, 2011-2012, 2012-2013. Write North to South, smallest to largest, largest to smallest, left to right.

Remember, if you give the audience something to read on a screen or in their hands, they will read it. So, let them. Give them time by pausing. When you rehearse, build in the time.

In the same way you talk them through the meaning or implications of a graph, map or chart, guide them through a slide with words by repeating the bullets on the screen. Others disagree. For me, though, when you speak the actual words, the audience both hears and sees them. Thus, you are reinforcing your ideas and increasing the odds of the audience's retaining the information. And because people read at different speeds, let them read the slide themselves before you say it out loud.

Keep your visuals simple. If you have "10 Reasons for Making Ireland a Tourist Destination" all on one slide, while you are talking about number two, the audience may be reading numbers nine and ten. You lose the reinforcement potential that way. Once again, consider using more slides, or presenting point one, then point one and two, then point one, two and three, and so on.

If you are presenting in person, when you are using visuals, again, remember you should not turn to the screen to look at them. Maintain eye contact. You do not abdicate that responsibility once you include images. If you are using a screen, remember to stand to one side. Should you want to, you need only turn quickly to look back to ensure that the audience is seeing what you want them to see.

If you are writing on a flipchart or whiteboard, avoid talking and writing at the same time. If you do, you will be projecting your voice at the board or onto the chart. Say the words and then turn to write or write and then turn back to the audience and say what you have written. And, if you are virtual, please avoid having one slide up for a prolonged period. Eyes tire. As do brains.

While we can binge watch a TV show, it's hard to stay focused on a fixed image on a computer screen.

And know the technology! Know its needs and foibles. In **Chapter 10**, when we talk about practicing, we will say more about this, but the point cannot be emphasized enough.

Earlier, we mentioned that people read whatever you distribute to them when you give it to them, unless you ask them not to do so – and that applies to chat as well. You can ask people to wait. If are using a handout at the beginning and know people will start reading, build that into your plan by saying, "If you look at the second point on the sheet, you will see that it indicates … ." Decide when to send a PDF. In other words, control what they do with what you have distributed. Because most people write on handouts, leave enough blank space for them to make notes.

Suppose, however, you want each member of the audience to have a copy of a complex table. Give it to them at the time that they need to refer to it and then tell them where you want them to look, "If you look at the third column, you will notice that it compares ... ."

To avoid problems, such as the third person in the fifth row not having received one, handouts are usually distributed at the end of a talk or are placed at each seat before the audience arrives.

Distribution of paper is another consideration. Will you ask others to help you? Will you hand one to each person individually or start at the end of a row? A time-consuming process either way.

If you opt for replicas or mock-ups, once again ask yourself, as you do with handouts or other visuals, what are you using them for and whether the audience will understand and benefit from their use.

In Summary

In other words, like so much of presenting you have a plethora of options from which to choose, from flip chart to video; the purpose is to clarify, underline and/or reinforce the message for the audience. They are not your notes!

Chapter 9
HANDLING QUESTIONS

'I'll answer some of your questions; the more difficult
ones will be answered by my colleagues."
**Professor Roland Smith, former Chairman,
British Aerospace plc**

Tired? You should be. You have done a lot of work, and
it is almost time for the show to begin. You have asked
questions, planned your talk and identified what, if any,
visual reinforcement or clarification is required. You
know what you are going to wear. Before you go out there
to face your public, consider another part of your talk:
the time when you have ended the prepared speech and
become the receiver. It is question time. In fact, some
presentations are all Q&A.

During your planning, you will have anticipated
questions and/or objections, and kept in mind the
political situation as well, so you should have a good
sense of people's perspectives. However, people will ask
what they want to ask. My single most important
recommendation is to try to maintain control of this part
of your talk. Avoid letting it slip away from you.

Knowing your subject as you do, any question about
the content should be no problem. A good way to prepare
is to practice by having a colleague or friend pose some
questions for you. When you answer the "How?" think
about the possibility of questions. Do you want

questions? And if so, when? Five minutes at the end? Or would you prefer to take some during the speech? If so, have you written yourself a note on your cards indicating that you need to tell the audience in the beginning that you will take questions during the talk? Maybe you have decided that questions will be over coffee, or that there will be no time for questions at all. Like so much else in a presentation, decide what works for the subject and for that audience.

Assume that you want to take questions and that, rather than use an interactive approach, you want all the questions held until the end. How much time have you allotted for them? Five minutes? Ten minutes? Whatever you have decided, stick to that time. It is easy to run long in this section because one question or answer may lead to three or four more, so keep an eye on the clock.

You have ended with a solid closing. You have restated your objective and called the audience to action: "Starting Tuesday, we will all be ..., because you can see

we will be saving at least 10%." Applause! Thank you!
Pause. Change of pace, perhaps you move to the right,
"Are there any questions?" or "I will be delighted to take
some questions" or "We have time for only three
questions." You invite them and do so with a smile. Avoid
looking defensive by crossing your arms on your chest
and taking two steps backward. Smile, step forward and
look open, eager and willing to take questions.

Take a moment and reflect on how it feels to be a
member of the audience during question time. We have
all been there. We spend time formulating the question,
finding the right words. Asking a question in a room full
of people is literally a mini-presentation. Those folks are
uncomfortable and need to be supported, so show
empathy please. How many times have we sat in an
audience wanting to ask a question, but reluctant to do
so, fearful that we will sound stupid or will say
something that reveals that we weren't listening? A
supervisor could be in the room seeing us make fools of
ourselves. With those memories in mind, be warm and
gracious to the questioner. No matter what you are
asked, help them retain their dignity. Don't expect their
gratitude, because they will not know that you are being
empathetic, but they will appreciate your kindness and
like you for it, which cannot hurt your cause.

While most people are diffident about asking
questions, others raise questions that have more to do
with their own need to be heard than they have to do
with your talk. A little posturing may be involved. How
often have you heard a question start with, "I just wanted
to say ..." and then go on at length and never ask
anything? If that happens, be sure that you are attentive.
There may be a question after the preamble. Hopefully,
you can avoid hurrying the person along, but you may

have to. Do not daydream or replay your talk. Listen. Use your skills – maintain eye contact, nod, if appropriate, to show that you are listening. Be sure you understand what is asked. You may have to say, "Do I understand you to mean ...?" Or you may want to repeat the question. Always bear in mind that what is said by someone in the front row may not have been heard at the back. Or you may want to paraphrase in words that are of your own choosing. If the questioner says, "Aren't the implications catastrophic?", you may want to select a less emotive word than "catastrophic," so you might say: "The implications have an impact ... ."

When you answer, begin by responding to the person who spoke; then continue by addressing the entire room. You have an obligation to everyone, and your response may give you the opportunity to support a point or clarify a misunderstanding. Avoid having a conversation or dialogue with one person who has "one more follow-up." However, if the question does reinforce your message, thank the individual for raising it, rather than looking disgusted.

In addition, try to keep each answer brief. If you have time for only three questions, you cannot devote the entire time to one. By the way, if you know someone's name, use it. Ask if there are more questions, wait briefly. If there are none, simply thank the audience again, smile and go. Once again, you make the decision to end the session.

If you do get a hostile audience member, avoid engaging in combat. Keep your answers on a higher plane. Restate your position. Usually, aggressive questioners will embarrass themselves.

Suppose you are asked a question, and you haven't a clue what the answer is. It happens. If you are concerned with maintaining your credibility, then do not talk around it. There is no available data on presenters who have been struck by a thunderbolt for not knowing the answers to every question; however, you can find out. Being able to locate information is an important skill, so admit that you do not know but that you can research it. Thank the individual for asking and promise to get back to them. And do.

If you have generated enthusiasm and an animated discussion ensues, maintain control. Suppose you do not have the answer to a question. Person A may offer to answer person B, and then person C might jump in. What happens is a discussion develops among the members of the audience, which may be wonderful, but unless you lead it like a conductor, you will be left standing, looking on. In other words, if you want A to talk to B and C to add something, be sure that you, not A, B, or C, are determining when they have said enough. *You* invite D to speak, not watch while D chimes in. When you decide that the debate has gone on long enough, *you* end it.

Sometimes, it is exciting to have the interaction move away from you, because it allows members of the audience to become involved. You may also get some useful feedback from what they are saying. And such interaction will indicate that you have sparked dialogue. Good for you! Do not discourage it; just orchestrate it and watch the clock.

In Summary

Your time is up. You may or may not want to restate your closing remarks. Hold your head high and look pleased with the event. Avoid rolling your eyes, dropping your shoulders and sighing. You are still on and being watched. Sit down, stop, leave the stage, or return to your seat with a sense of accomplishment.

Chapter 10
REHEARSING

"Practice is everything."
Diogenes Laertius, Greek historian

Handling questions, like every other aspect of presentation requires practice, and finding the time to do so is up to you. This chapter is about practicing. No coach can run the marathon or play the match for the athletes. Once you have your talk thought out and the key points on your cue cards, even if the visuals are not completed, start running through what you plan to say from beginning to end.

Because you rehearse your talk in part for timing, use your watch, find a clock, or set your phone and start from the very beginning, including your "Good morning" or "Good afternoon." Say it out loud, grope for the missing word, use your examples, tell your stories, take pauses and, as you do, think about where your visuals will be and start building in the pauses when you know that the audience will be looking at them.

If you recite the talk only in your head, without the pause for the answer to a hypothetical question, or for the laugh, or for the slides, your timing may be off. Those little additions take time. As you say the words aloud, you also discover what words should be emphasized. You may want to underline them on the cards or draw parallel lines between them to indicate a pause after a key point.

You also may realize that, as you hear what you are saying, that some data needs to be added, clarified or deleted. Or you may feel that you have too many arguments supporting one point, or that one of your arguments is too weak to be included, or that something that recently occurred in the office or in the world might be a good example to include, or you may need transitions to move you from point to point.

Practicing takes time and is an integral part of the process of refining the speech and your delivery. Carry your notes with you, and whenever you have time, take them out of your pocket, bag or briefcase – or look at your phone – and read them to increase your comfort level.

The Room

If you are in person, look at the room. When you asked the question "Where?" in your preparation, you may have been given a description of the venue or you could see it online. Regardless, walk around the room to get a feel for its idiosyncrasies. In effect, you are on reconnaissance, and you enter with all your antennae absorbing information. What are the acoustics like? Is there an echo? Heavy drapes and carpets or none? Is the view distracting? Can you close the shades? Where are the cords or buttons? Will heavy fabric absorb your voice? Speak out loud. Will your voice be heard in the back, or will you need to use a mic, and if so, when will you have an opportunity to practice with it? What kind do they have? Which do you prefer?

What about the furniture? Tables and chairs? Are there only chairs? Do you need tables? Who provides them? When? What are the seats like? Straight-backed and hard, or deeply cushioned with wheels – the easier to relax in, snooze in, or roll about in? How is the room arranged? Are the chairs, or can they be moved? Do you want the room in theatre-style, classroom-style, or would you prefer a U-shape? The advantage of a U-shape is that there are fewer barriers between you and the audience. The audience, too, can eyeball each other, not stare at the back of a neighbor's head.

What is at the front of the room for you? Is there a table, a lectern? Are they movable or fixed? Will there be a head table? How big is it? Can you move around it with ease? Will it be covered by a cloth, or are your legs and feet clearly visible to the audience? How high will the table or lectern be? Can you be seen over it? Remember the pictures of Queen Elizabeth in Washington DC, some years ago? Only her head and hat appeared over the lectern. Someone had forgotten to check the facilities before she started her speech.

What are the sight lines? In other words, when you are standing in the front of the room, if every seat were filled could you be seen from every angle? Is there a pillar or a piece of equipment that blocks your view and theirs? Do you need to move chairs back or prevent people from sitting in certain seats? If you are using a computer, where can you put it? If you are using a flipchart, where does it need to be placed for you to write comfortably and for the audience to see? Left- or right-handedness determines where to position it. Are there enough pads for the flip chart? Pens, markers, pointers, erasers, chalk – what do you need to bring with you? Where are the light switches? How dark is the room with or without lights?

Can people take notes? Or bring their laptops? Are there cables across the floor? Is there Wi-Fi? Could you trip? Where are the electrical outlets? Do you need additional extension cords? Can you record and playback?

Will the technology work? Are you familiar with their system? Is there an IT person available to set up? Can you manage without? Where are the power buttons? The volume control? The remote controls? Which button controls what? Is there someone other than yourself who could press some buttons? Is there room at the speaker's table for your laptop and a glass of water?

Is where you are walking carpeted or will every footfall echo? Should you change your choice of shoes?

Are there windows? Is the room draughty? What is visible outside? Will people be walking by? Is there heavy truck traffic? How public are you? Can the windows be opened or shut? How warm is the room when doors are closed? Warm enough for people to become sleepy? Are there telephones? Will they ring? Can they be disconnected? Are there loudspeakers that will make the room sound like an airport or hospital? Can you control them? Are there doors that people in an outside corridor may inadvertently open?

Details. Details. Details. Sound like a lot of work? It isn't really, perhaps only 10 or 15 minutes. You are checking for possible problems, and increasing your own comfort level in the same way a dog or cat does before snuggling down into his or her favorite spot.

The Introductions

When you rehearse, it is not all about the technology, tables, and chairs. There are human elements to be considered as well. Will you be introducing yourself, or will someone else do that? If it is someone else, what do you want them to say – or not say – about you or your talk? Sometimes an introduction by another person can take a good line from your talk or misstate your purpose, so agree in advance. Where will that person be sitting? Where will you be in relation to that individual? What is the person's name? Can you pronounce it? Will that person lead any post-talk questions, or will you? Will they or you make concluding remarks?

If you are wondering if there are rules about all this, if one way is better than another, or if one method is right and another wrong, the answer is "No." It is right, if it is right for you and for what you are trying to achieve. If you have thought through the implications of your decisions, and you are comfortable, then it is the appropriate approach.

Wondering why you should bother? Looking poised and at ease is more impressive than rushing into a room saying, "Where do I speak from?" or "When do I start?"

or fiddling with the computer or tapping on a mic. Your audience may not know when you have done your homework, but they will know when you have not. There are enough spontaneous events that may occur during your talk, so why clutter your mind on the day with extraneous details like locating switches that could have been found in advance in just a few minutes?

Team Presentations

Another aspect to your practicing and planning that you should consider relates to your being a member of a team presentation. There is no difference in your planning except that you will have asked the questions together or shared answers so that you all have a clear sense of your brief. If you are working in a team, divide the labor in advance. Decide who is speaking on what aspect and in what order, compare notes on the data that each of you may be using and on the approach that each of you is taking.

A team presentation is not a team presentation just because three or four people happen to be talking. It involves teamwork in its truest sense. The unique talents of the members of a pro basketball squad are not brought together on the afternoon of a game without an opportunity for the players to practice together and know the plays in advance.

When speaking, get used to each other's presentation styles, strengths, weaknesses and how best to use or diffuse them. Determine if there is too much or too little overlap or none. Unless you talk among yourselves, one of you may make assumptions that the other person is handling an important aspect that, in fact, is not being handled at all.

As a team, you also need to plan your introductions. Will one of you be explaining who is going to say what: "John will address the long-range plans, while I will be describing the current ones." Or will each of you introduce yourselves as you go along? How will you "hand the baton" from one to the next? Plan the question period too. Which one of you will be taking which questions? Will one of you take all of them, or will you divide them up, depending on the focus? And if someone is hit with a tough question, what's the support system?

Also, decide about the seating or standing arrangements. Will each of you walk up from the audience or be at a table? During the questions will you all be standing? And how will you refer to each other; "My colleague, Bill" or "Bill." Will you be "handing over" to Bill, or will you have a sentence that reintroduces Bill's section, for example, "Bill, will now discuss the reasons for ..." or "Bill is better able to ... ."

Know that the audience is watching everyone on the team, not only the speaker of the moment. It is remarkable how often in a team presentation the members look unhappy. Be sure to listen when your colleagues speak. Even if you are tired of working with each other, give the impression that you get on together, and that you care about each other. You do that by looking at the other person and being involved in and reacting to what your teammate is saying. If there is a joke, smile at it. If one of you makes a mistake, the other one should be ready to pick up. When your eyes are on the speaker of the moment, the audience will focus too. Avoid looking away or checking your notes. That applies to remote teams as well.

In Summary

In other words, practicing is about getting comfortable with the material and with your environment to free you from unnecessary anxieties. Build in the time to run through your talk to refine and time it and visit the room even if it means an additional trip. Once there, examine the layout and the equipment carefully. If there are others involved, talk with them to ensure that the presentation runs smoothly.

Chapter 11
PRESENTING ONLINE

"Brevity is the soul of wit."
William Shakespeare, playwright

Your charm, your enthusiasm, your commitment to your subject and to your audience is unchanged when you present virtually. While some of your audiences may be live, in most instances, both you and they are virtual, and they may only see you from the waist up. I once asked a virtual group what they had on their feet -- most admitted to socks, no shoes.

Bear in mind that if they are on their computers, they may be experiencing Zoom fatigue, or if they are working from home, they may be uncomfortable because of the chairs they are sitting in or the computer set-ups they have. They may have buffering connections, or delightful pets, or energetic offspring. In other words, your audience's environment or physical discomfort may affect their ability to concentrate on what you are saying. Even in the office, folks may walk by a cubicle or stop to say "Hello" without realizing that you are online.

With that said, be sure to maintain your eye contact, your enthusiasm and keep track of time. Try to make your content as tight as possible. If you know your presentation must be long to cover the essential material, then find ways to break it up by giving your audience something to do; send them into break-out rooms to talk to each other to consider an issue or take a short break for them to stretch and let the blood circulate. If they are exhausted, and if this is virtual meeting number four for the day, they may be unable to listen and process what you are saying.

When you are speaking, be sure that you are positioned so that you are looking at the camera and that there is only a small amount of space between you and the top of the screen. I am sure that you have been in enough virtual meetings by now to have seen some speakers with superb posture and other folks with only the tops of their heads showing or only a profile. Do whatever you can to angle your computer or yourself, so you are sitting tall, face front with a limited amount of space between you and the upper frame.

Consider the lighting. If you are working from home or from the office, check to see whether you are in darkness or in glare. Neither one serves you. Again, without investing in ergonomic chairs and special lighting at home, modify or work with what you have. Can you move a light? Can you shut or open the blinds? You simply want enough light for people to see your face clearly.

Like lighting, your choice of clothing is as important as it is for all presentations, but in this instance, solid colors serve you better. Blue happens to be a good choice. Steer away from patterns or plaids or dramatic color combinations that may take on a life of their own on the computer. Your animated face is what matters. (And, yes, there is Zoom make up available. Let me leave it at that.)

And like your clothing, the choice of background should also be understated. Some folks enjoy a background of palm trees or appearing to be inside space capsules or sitting next to a famous landmark like Stonehenge or Old Faithful Geyser in Yellowstone National Park. As charming or nostalgic as those images may be, like moving stripes on your shirt or blouse, they are distracting. As an audience member, I may begin planning my next holiday while I should be concentrating on the implications of a new policy. To this day, I still remember the golden retriever puppies in the red wagon – I have absolutely no recollection of the content of the meeting. The reverse is also true. If your choice is too stark, it can also be off putting. I recall one meeting where the speaker was in a white room with a white desk. Rather than concentrating on staffing issues, I found myself thinking of *One Flew Over the Cuckoo's Nest*. In other words, find the balance between stark and overly cute and whatever you opt for, your face rather than the background should be the focus.

If you are using slides on a shared screen, please design your visuals as we discussed earlier, as simply and as clearly as possible. A cluttered slide is as difficult to read on a computer as it is in person. Keep your slides simple, and please take them down as soon as possible after you have referred to them. Staring at a slide for umpteen minutes with a voice in the background is fatiguing. Although most of us admit to binge watching at home or to sitting comfortably in a movie theater for several hours, that visual experience is different because the images change quickly. We see scenes from multiple angles. We see a profile, a closeup, a long shot. On a computer watching a presentation, we are staring at a face and possibly a pair of hands and perhaps a slide or two or even a video clip. To keep your audience interested in what you are saying, your face and your voice and your enthusiasm or warmth coming through the screen are vital to the success of your presentation.

In Summary

One of the best ways to prepare for your own virtual meeting is to look at other presenters in meetings that you attend online. What distracts you in their background? What backgrounds are too clever? What annoys you? What facial expression is easy on the eye? What colors do you like? Experiment. And remember because technology is technology is technology, write down the call-in number, so if a crash occurs, you are able to resume as quickly as possible, and be ready to make essential slides available *via* a PDF.

Chapter 12
HANDLING YOUR NERVES

"You have no reason to fear the wind if your hay-
bales are tied down."
Irish proverb

"Considering how dangerous everything is,
nothing is really very frightening."
Gertrude Stein

Now that the time for your presentation is nearing, you
may be experiencing some doubts. This chapter is
devoted to your worries and offers some thoughts about
handling them. First, accept that you will always be
nervous before you talk. Stage fright is normal. A little
adrenaline energizes the team, the athlete, the dancer or
the speaker. There is no reason to be ashamed or
embarrassed. For most people, nervousness does not
last long into the performance; it fades quickly. However,
to understand your own "fight or flight" response, it is
helpful once again to become more self-aware. In other
words, learn to recognize your own reactions when you
are under stress and then accept or compensate for
them. By doing so, you diminish them.

The best cure for nerves, if there is one, is to do your
homework so that you are prepared. The better you
know the material, the audience, the venue, the less

anxious you will be. Running through your material in advance also increases your comfort level. In addition, rather than berating yourself for feeling nervous, remember that everyone becomes anxious, not just you. We are all affected by the jitters in different ways.

In workshops, people have told me that, before speaking, their palms or underarms are drenched with sweat. Some begin to feel their hearts pounding in their chests. Remember the expression, "My heart was in my mouth"? Others have "hollow feelings" in the pits of their stomachs. Others feel heat around their faces, and their necks are flushed. Still others feel the strength ebb from their legs, their hands tremble; in some folk, throats go dry. Some need the bathroom more often. Do you recognize any of these symptoms? If you do, you have also noticed that the sensations ease as you gain control of your body and of the situation early in your talk.

Please note that this chapter is called "Handling your Nerves," not "Curing your Nerves." Again, accept the fact that some nervousness is normal; however, these techniques may ease the symptoms or at least help you compensate for them.

For example, many people find that having a cup of tea or coffee before giving a talk helps them to focus. It may. It also may heighten their anxiety. Eliminating caffeine is one of the first suggestions for people who fear flying. Coffee is also a diuretic, so you may find yourself going off to the toilet one more time. Consider having only what you need to avoid a headache and foregoing that extra cup or two. That is particularly true if you have a sensitive stomach. Instead have some room-temperature water – not ice water - near where you are speaking. This is even more important if you know that your mouth goes dry. The water also helps the adrenaline move through your body. By the way, taking a sip is also a great excuse for a well-timed pause. If your legs do not feel as if they will support you, be sure that you know the route that takes you from where you are sitting to where you are speaking. Practice walking the path, especially if there are steps to climb or descend. If there is a banister, hold on to it.

Suppose your fear, though, is that you are going to panic and forget everything you planned to say. Although we talked in **Chapter 7** about using notes, it is important to mention their use here. The day that I went blank in front of the camera, I had no notes. I learned a lesson. I use notes. As I suggested earlier, consider writing down your opening sentences word for word on a card. If you have worked yourself into a state of panic, as I had, the precise words will be written there so you know why you are speaking and what the subject is. As you ease into the next few sentences, the anxiety will fade. I promise.

Because we are most uneasy at the outset, you may want to take the attention off yourself by creating a diversion, by designing an opening that moves the focus from you to something else. For example, you might ask the audience to "talk to your neighbor" briefly about an activity you have planned, or you might have a visual projected on the screen or have a question pre-flipped, on a white board, in the chat box, or on a slide. By doing that you involve the audience in the activity or have them looking at something other than at you.

There are other calming techniques as well. It is important to remember that you are knocking the stuffing out of yourself with your self-doubts. Remember the answer to "Why me?" Because "We know you can do it," "You know more about the topic than anyone else," etc. Make a list of your accomplishments and keep it handy. Refer to it in advance of any stressful situation. You may say that you do not have any achievements, but you do: earning your diploma, going to another country and getting a job on your own, winning a particular game, finishing a particular project, or earning a promotion. We are not looking for lists that start off with "winning the Nobel Prize." Just list things that you are proud of and that made you feel good. In advance of the speech, recall the list to remind yourself that you are a winner. What you are doing is replacing negative thoughts with positive ones.

Also, consider taking a moment or two to go off on your own to calm yourself. Close your eyes and visualize a tranquil place or moment that you have experienced, perhaps a deserted beach, or a quiet forest, or the water of a lake gently lapping against the shore. By closing your eyes and concentrating on that peaceful scene, you may relax. Neuroscientists say that daydreaming for a few minutes every hour is an excellent habit to cultivate, given our current information overload.

Be sure to take some deep breaths, inhaling through your nose and exhaling slowly through your mouth – a good idea when you are about to speak. It is also one of the reasons why you should stand tall with your chest up. Good posture allows you to fill your lungs. Not only does it improve your voice; those deep breaths, rather than shallow ones, are calming. So, do not begin until you are ready, and you have taken several deep breaths.

If you are still making yourself crazy, choose one self-doubt and follow it to its natural conclusion. In other words, if you hear the internal tape say, "I will be terrible!" focus on it and start analyzing it. "Well, now, what will be terrible? Why? Then what will happen to me if it is? And then what?" Force your mind to address the thought and take it to a realistic outcome. If you do, you will see that the outcomes are usually unrealistic. You are not going to die, be ostracized, exiled, imprisoned or laid off, nor will the ground open and swallow you whole.

Why not try the reverse? Tell yourself that all will go well, that the audience will be supportive and that the technology will work. Recent research suggests that standing and putting your hands on your hips prior to speaking – taking a power pose – sends a message to your brain that you are OK and in charge. In essence, try to ease the stress with positive physical and mental activities.

In Summary

Treat speaking nerves the way you do stress of any kind; the recommendations are the same: besides positive self-talk and deep breathing, finding a few minutes to stretch your legs helps too. Rather than pace in the hall or in your office, take a brisk 10-minute walk. Being at home may give you more options.

Chapter 13
IT'S SHOW TIME!

"The ability to speak is a short cut to distinction. It puts a man in the limelight, raises him head and shoulders above the crowd, and the man who can speak acceptably is usually given credit for an ability out of all proportion to what he really possesses."

Lowell Thomas, American journalist

You have done your planning, asked your questions and written the material. You are looking good: shoes shining, hair trimmed, notes in hand, visuals in order, thoughts positive. It's show time! But you are not quite finished. Do you recall the initial recommendation to make decisions before, during and after a talk?

Suppose your talk is part of a lengthier discussion, or you are one of a series of speakers. Then, on the day, try to attend other sessions to hear what the other presenters' views are. In that way you can modify your own speech based on what you hear someone else say. For example, you may find that you disagree or agree with or like a particular phrase that was used, or realize that they have said what you have planned to say, so you can use it: "As Brendan said earlier ..." or "As Kim said, I must disagree that ..." or "There is no need for me to explain what Malcolm stated so clearly but ... ." Besides looking professional, you are role-modeling good listening skills for your audience.

In addition, on the day of your talk be aware of any noteworthy, relevant items in the news, perhaps a major economic event, a sports trade, a literary award, a national election or 100 mile per hour winds. You might be able to incorporate one of these occurrences into the opening of your talk or as an analogy or example. Doing that may bring your message home once again or bring it to life.

You have completed the planning and anticipating what you can. It is time to think on your feet, to handle whatever happens spontaneously as it occurs, to make instantaneous decisions. Some you might have anticipated; others you will not.

Imagine you have been introduced. You have begun – the audience is with you, all is well, but you make a mistake, or something happens in the room. You lose your place, slip on a word, or drop one of your cards. Or the microphone squeals, the video connection becomes wonky. What should you do? The audience may welcome the notion that you are human, and as humans, we are fallible, so rather than trying to cover it, make the mistake and make it big. Smile, laugh, apologize. Then, collect your thoughts, say the word correctly, bend down and pick up the card, adjust the microphone or have the number to call in. You may even be able to incorporate some aspect of the error into your talk. Then let it go. It happened, and it is over. Like a missed basket or a net ball, there is another point to play. If you dwell on the error, you risk another one. What does every sports announcer say? "__ has lost concentration." Regain yours.

Now suppose you are well into your talk, and several people enter the room late. Make an assessment. If you see members of the audience turning to look at or comment to the newcomer(s), you have lost their attention. Stop. Look pleasant. No point looking annoyed. Why make them feel more uncomfortable than they probably already are? Diffuse their discomfort with a smile. You are looking for friends, not enemies. Once they are settled, continue. Depending on how many or who, you may want to make a one or two sentence recap or indicate that "We were making the point that ... ."

Well, you have had your error and your interruption. It would be nice to believe that you now can switch on automatic pilot. Sadly you can't. Recall what we said about eye contact: about looking and seeing what is happening? Take in the smiles, frowns, glazed eyes, doodling, surfing on the laptop, side conversations, or surreptitious cell phone checking. If you sense that the audience is fatiguing, make a change.

Based on your own repertoire of talents, vary what you have been doing. This shift of tempo is like a symphony, with movements written in different tempos. Maybe it is time to walk or to move quickly. Maybe you have not played with your voice at all, so it is time to change the volume, to take it down to a whisper or to raise it to a shout. Do you think what you have been saying is too complicated or abstract? When did you notice the audience starting to fade? Is it time for a quick recap, for an example or anecdote? Should you open a window? Turn down the thermostat? Should you take a break? Should you eliminate an upcoming section that you had planned to discuss? Should you take questions? Should you move to a breakout session?

In other words, based on what is happening, do something different. What you choose is entirely up to you. By watching and gauging reactions and by making changes, you will keep the presentation energized and the audience engaged. With your audience uppermost in your thoughts, you will be reacting to them and keeping them with you.

And When It's Over ...

You have done it! Bask in the applause. Sure, be relieved, enjoy the moment and be proud of your effort. The audience will let you know that you did a good job. They may not appreciate all the work that you put into preparation, but you have succeeded. Like any professional, you made it look seamless and easy.

When the presentation is over, you will be tired. Maintaining that degree of concentration during a talk is fatiguing. But while the event is fresh in your mind, replay your own mental tape of the proceedings. Do not be hypercritical: "Oh, I put my hand in my pocket four times"; "I said 'er' too often," "I looked at one side of the room too much," "I meant to … ." OK, you did. But what went right? Accept that old habits will give way to new and better ones, so look at the big picture. Did the opening work? Were your arguments clear? Did the questions suggest that the audience understood your message, or were all the questions on one aspect? What does that tell you?

Ask for some feedback from others in addition to relying on your own self-assessment. We are our "own worst critics." And ask for specific feedback – more than "Great job!" or "Awesome!" Find out what people liked and what worked. Listen to what people recall. Is it what you want them to remember? Add this data to your wealth of approaches that work for you or that may not. Learn from what you did to apply it to the next talk. Experiment.

In addition to your own self-assessment and feedback from friends, colleagues, and attendees, observe other people. Watch other speakers. Look at the way successful businessmen and women dress, look at their hair, their color combinations, their choice of backgrounds, the fit of their clothes, their choice of jewelry. Look at TED Talks, TV, YouTube, the news, webinars, and watch movies.

Every time you sit in a meeting, watch the speaker, notice their movements, their speech pattern, their facial expressions, their use of their hands, how they cope with mistakes, how they deal with questions, what visuals they use, what new technologies they tested. Ask yourself whether it worked – for you and for the audience in general. Pay attention and listen to the audience. Develop a critical eye about what appears to be effective and what is not. Start saving stories or anecdotes for future reference.

Look for excuses to speak again. Every time you stand up and speak, you hone your skills. At the end of the day, you should see talking to an audience – live or remote – as an opportunity for you and your organization to shine. You have a platform to convince others, to change thinking – an opportunity – one that is more influential than believing that you are experiencing a fate second only to dying.

In Summary

Given our increasingly technological society, being able to speak to others, to give a good presentation is a marketable skill in today's competitive global business environment. Whether you are an entrepreneur in pursuit of funding, a political activist seeking support, or a member of a multinational explaining new strategies, a person who can prepare and deliver an effective talk is an asset. Someone who can sell, motivate, persuade, tell, encourage and/or entertain others is invaluable, because such people make social change, win new business, encourage staff, explain ideas, articulate problems, present alternatives and justify decisions. And when they do, people listen.

You can be such a person if you consider the recommendations and practice techniques to enhance your skills. You may still say to yourself, "I'll be OK," "I'll be fine," "It will be over soon," but you will be no longer an individual filled with anxiety. You will be speaking from a position of knowledge and strength. The emphasis changes, because I have no doubt that "Yes, you will be OK; you will be fine!" – more than OK and more than fine. Unlike athletes and dancers who age, as a speaker, you become more effective, credible, confident and clear. For you, undoubtedly, there will be another day and another talk.

ABOUT THE AUTHOR

Elizabeth P. Tierney, PhD is a writer, trainer, consultant and lecturer in Communications and Management. She was a school administrator in the US and taught at University College Dublin, Ireland, Cesuga in Spain and Willamette University in Oregon.

She coaches and delivers workshops, speaks at conferences and is the author of 14 books. *Word Time! A Guide to Effective Writing,* a companion to *Show Time!,* will be published by Oak Tree Press in 2023.

9 781781 195611